THE HOME-BUILDING KIT CATALOG

THE HOME-BUILDING KIT CATALOG

A DIRECTORY AND SOURCE BOOK

BY MIKE McCLINTOCK

HARMONY BOOKS/NEW YORK

Published by Harmony Books, a division of Crown Publishers, Inc., One Park Avenue, New York, New York 10016 and simultaneously in Canada by General Publishing Company Limited

HARMONY and colophon are trademarks of Crown Publishers, Inc.

Manufactured in the United States of America

Library of Congress Cataloging in Publication Data

McClintock, Michael, 1945–
  The home-building kit catalog.

  Includes index.
  1. Prefabricated houses—Catalogs.   I. Title.
TH4819.P7M3 1985   693′.97   85-5429
ISBN 0-517-55585-9
10 9 8 7 6 5 4 3 2 1
First Edition

CONTENTS

THE HOME-BUILDING KIT CATALOG

INTRODUCTION

What Is a Prefab Home?

Prefab means you don't have to start from scratch. A home manufacturer prepares the house in some way before it gets to the building site. Such components as 2 x 4 studs, particleboard counters, and many other building materials are technically prefab, because they are preformed parts of a house. But you have to figure out where they go, cut them, and put them in place. The prefab homes in this book offer a lot more than that.

Some prefabs are called turnkey homes. They are precut, pre-wired, preassembled, and prebuilt in every way possible. All do-it-yourselfers or owner-builders have to do is turn the key in the front door lock. But most prefab firms let you participate, if you want to, at many different stages of construction. For example, a company that precuts Colonial timber frame homes might sell a frame-only package that you or your contractor install. A typical second option would include the frame plus roofing, siding, and windows and doors—all the materials needed to create a complete house shell.

Some firms offer labor and materials with every option. Some offer design and planning services and leave the physical work to you. A typical third package offering, which is almost turnkey building, would include interior finishing materials as well as the structure and closed-in shell: paneling, wallboard, closet shelves, interior doors, and more.

Trailer Park Images

A Colonial timber frame does not fit the mobile home image tradi-tionally associated with prefab construction and manufactured housing. Houses built wholly or in part at the factory, then trucked to the site, were once small, metal-sided cigar boxes with peculiar little built-in cupboards and appliances.

But even mobile homes, now called manufactured or site-delivered homes, aren't what they used to be. Many are built in 28-foot widths, with wood-burning fireplaces and vaulted ceilings. The technology used to mass-produce manufactured housing is now flexible enough to produce many different styles and sizes. In fact, many manufactured-housing firms offer thirty, forty, or fifty standard plans, and allow a wide degree of modification to floor plans and materials inside and out.

Slowly but surely, the benefits of mass-produced housing have been applied to more homes in more sizes in more architectural styles. One manufacturing firm, Marley Continental Homes, which offers a series of standard ranch and raised ranch, development-type houses, has just introduced a new line with extensive Victorian detailing. They are not historically accurate reproductions, yet the floor plans are traditional. The facades are loaded with intricate moldings, curved shakes, two-story connecting bay windows, and many other features you might find on an old town house. But these "Victorian" homes don't need massive renovation. They are brand-new, energy-efficient, built at the factory, and delivered to the site in sections.

Mass production and precutting need not produce boring little boxes. In these pages you'll find many types of houses. One of the most popular kinds is log homes, from small, rustic cabins to huge, 4,000-square-foot monsters, built with many different kinds of logs. Some companies offer highly machined logs, even composite log walls with insulating foam cores. Others offer hand-peeled, full-round, massive 18-inch-diameter logs with precut but traditional saddle-notched corners.

There are solid cedar timber homes, post and beam homes, sun-room additions, Colonial reproductions, all kinds of low-cost panelized homes, and prefab earth-sheltered homes. There are even completely finished turnkey vacation homes shaped like flying saucers, which rest on elevated pedestal-base foundations. All are prepared to a large degree by the manufacturer, making owner building a realistic possibility.

Dealing with Prefab Companies

A house might seem like the last thing you should buy through the mail sight unseen. Most prefab firms recognize this problem and prepare elaborate information kits for consumers. You can usually get a brief, reasonably comprehensive flier free on request. The full presentations often cost $5, $6, or even $10, but they do provide an extremely detailed look at the firm's products.

But before you order, realize that you are likely to get much more than you need to satisfy your idle curiosity. A typical package from a large company might have a fifty- or eighty-page full-color booklet with photos and floor plans of fifty or more models, design guidelines, details of materials and construction, booklets on case histories of owner-builders, energy-efficiency calculations, reprints of magazine articles, and more—a mass of materials designed to overcome any reluctance to order by mail.

If you elect to shop regionally you'll save on shipping. Also, you can take a day to visit the plant, get your hands on some of the materials, and sit down with company personnel. Larger firms have an advantage in this regard, as many work through a national network of franchised dealers. The headquarters office can provide you with a reasonably local name, someone you can check out and talk to face-to-face.

The firms in this book are from all parts of the country. All were contacted, and responded with details about sizes and styles and materials and costs that you can read about in the individual en-tries. Many have toll-free (800) numbers you can call for information.

The associations listed below can provide more information on the industry, and lists of their member firms if you would like to investigate more companies on your own. But you will find a full, representative selection of prefab homes here—from very basic, inexpensive shelters to expansive and luxurious homes in virtually every architectural style.

Canadian Home Manufacturers
  Association
27 Goulburn Avenue
Ottawa, Ontario, Canada K1N 8C7

Canadian Logbuilders Association
Box 403
Prince George, British Columbia,
  Canada V2L 4S2

North American Log Builders
  Association
P.O. Box 369
Lake Placid, NY 12946

Manufactured Housing Institute
1745 Jefferson Davis Highway
Arlington, VA 22202

Home Manufacturers Council
National Association of
  Home Builders
15th and M streets NW
Washington, DC 20005

Solar Greenhouse Association
34 N. Gore
Webster Groves, MO 63110

U.S. Department of Housing and
  Urban Development
Manufactured Housing Standards
  Division
Washington, DC 20410

GLOSSARY OF TERMS AND ABBREVIATIONS

Anchor A bolt with a protruding threaded stem set in a concrete or block wall. Anchors are used to tie a wooden sill to the foundation.

AWWF An acronym for All-Weather Wood Foundation, a system using wooden, pressure-treated sills, plates, studs, and underground plywood sheathing in place of a conventional masonry foundation. This economical system is quickly and easily installed in any type of weather, even in severe cold, which can curtail masonry work.

Berm A small knoll made of earth, generally man-made terrain, which is mounded to shelter a house.

Broken-back rafter A roof line common on many colonial homes in which the slope of the main roof is decreased, for example, where a porch or shed extension joins the main house.

Butt and pass A common corner design system for log homes, in which one log butts up against another that passes the first log and overhangs the wall.

Checking Sometimes mistaken for splitting, checking is an opening along the wood grain, almost as though the grain had been unzipped. It is usually caused by seasoning as the wood dries.

Closed in The point in construction when the building frame is covered with sheathing (not necessarily finished siding and trim), with windows and doors set into their openings. Technically, the roof deck closes in the frame, although this term is commonly

taken to mean protected against the weather, and therefore includes finished roofing.

Course One row of material, for example, a layer of concrete block or brick, or a row of shingles.

Crosstie Also called a collar beam, this timber connects two sides of the triangle formed where roof rafters meet, completing an A-shape. It stiffens the frame and reduces the outward thrust force of sloped rafters.

Dimensional timber The normal assortment of structural lumber in stock at most lumber yards, generally 2 x 4s to 2 x 12s.

Dovetail corner A construction method in which interlacing elements meet at right angles. It is used in all types of construction from joints of dresser drawers to the corners of log cabins.

Engineered construction While virtually every building is now erected with some form of an engineering plan, this term describes modern, minimal framing in which the emphasis is on getting more structural strength out of less wood, for example, by using trusses.

Fraction dome Refers to the part, proportion, or fraction of the whole dome sphere that sits on the foundation. For example, a 3/8-fraction dome is less than half the sphere and slightly flat looking, while a 5/8-fraction dome is more than half the sphere and slightly egg-shaped.

Gambrel A double-pitched roof in which the upper rafter is gently

sloped to provide headroom inside, and the lower rafter is steeply sloped down to the studwall.

Kiln-dried Lumber that is dried in an oven to remove moisture. While most framing timbers have a 19 percent moisture content, kiln-drying reduces this percentage to make timbers (particularly trim and frames) more stable and less apt to warp and twist.

Light window Expressed as a number of lights, such as nine-light, or 6/6 light, which refers to the number of individual panes of glass in the unit; 6/6 means 6 panes above 6 panes.

Mass gain A principle of heat storage that relates the size and storage capacity of any building material to the heat (and sometimes the cooling, when considering air conditioning) it stores and reradiates. For example, it has been shown that solid log walls, even without fiber glass insulation, store a great deal of heat in the mass of wood fibers, then release the heat back into the living space when the air cools.

On center A building layout system in which wall studs, floor joists, and rafters are installed with a specific distance (either 16 or 24 inches) from the center of one to the other. This system allows other building materials such as plywood sheathing to fit from timber to timber without waste.

Panelized A construction method in which large wall sections are fabricated off the site, under controlled conditions, where many stages of construction may be completed. Exterior sheathing, windows and doors, even interior wallboard and trim may be added to the panel, which is then fitted into a structural system at the site.

Passive solar Architectural features that take advantage of solar heating, for example, overhangs that allow winter sun to hit windows while excluding summer sun. Passive designs do not include mechanical systems such as solar collectors.

Plate The top horizontal member in a studwall. The bottom timber is often called a shoe.

Plenum A chamber, generally adjacent to a heating plant, from which individual ducts carry conditioned air to rooms. One innovative system, called Plen-Wood, uses the entire crawl space beneath the floor joists as a giant distribution plenum.

Post and beam A framing system using timbers larger than conventional 2 x 4s, and farther apart from each other than standard 16- or 24-inch centers. Typically 4 x 4s are set 4 feet on center and are spanned by timbers 2 x 6 or larger.

Purlin A timber running at right angles to the roof rafters. Typically used on roof frames where rafters are set more than 24 inches on center, particularly truss frame roofs.

Ridge The highest point or peak of a roof, generally formed by a timber running from one end of the building to the other against which rafters are fixed at right angles.

R-value A measure of resistance to heat transmission; for example, in insulation products. The higher the R-value, the more effective the insulation.

Saddle-notch A system of interlacing logs in which a saucer-shaped cutout of roughly half the log diameter enables the logs to join at right angles.

Shiplap A type of siding lumber in which the edges are cut thinner than the main plank so that one board overlaps another at the joint.

Spline A connector used to join two pieces of material that butt against each other; a common feature of kit log homes where a thin strip of material is set into grooves aligned in the wall logs to seal out the weather and prevent shifting.

Stick built Conventional framing that uses 2 x 4 wall studs and individual pieces of lumber set one at a time.

Stress skin panel A modern system of manufacturing prefabricated wall sections (or roof sections) that include sheathing, even windows and doors, but less than the conventional number of framing members. Some stress skin panels eliminate all timbers and substitute a corrugated stiffener between exterior and interior surfaces, or a solid foam core that enhances insulation.

T&G Abbreviation for *tongue and groove joint system*. In a T&G system, one edge of a board is grooved and the other is cut with a raised center section along the edge that fits into the groove in an adjacent board. The T&G joint usually includes a slight bevel along the edge.

Thermal break An insulated interruption in solid materials, for example, a strip of vinyl or rigid foam in an aluminum window frame that separates cold exterior metal from transmitting temperatures directly through to the inside surface.

Turnkey Homes prefabricated to the point that buyers only have to turn the key in the door before moving in. Virtually all materials, including drapes, rugs, and light fixtures are included in the sales package.

U-factor A complex method of determining the energy efficiency of construction. As opposed to R-factors for specific building materials, the U-factor includes R-values, dead air spaces, and the configuration of materials in the wall to produce a realistic rating.

Water table An angled sill at windows and some doors with a shelf cut into the thickness of the sill, which prevents leaks.

WR, FC wallboard These two notations stand for different types of specialized gypsum wallboard: WR for "water-resistant," and FC for "fire code."

LOG HOMES

AIR-LOCK LOG COMPANY, INC.

P.O. Box 2506
Las Vegas, NM 87701
(505) 425-8888

PRODUCT RANGE

Air-Lock manufactures a range of homes from 288-square-foot cabins to large custom hotel buildings, all from their unique, center-drilled logs. Each log has a hole bored through the center for controlled drying, less checking and cracking. Nearly sixty standard floor plans are offered, and the company will precut logs for any custom plan.

PREFAB COMPONENTS

Standard packages include all 6-inch center-drilled wall logs, pre-cut for window and door openings with 12-inch corner extensions, interior log walls on most plans, gable end full logs, solid, peeled rafter logs and tie beams, log purlins and trusses good for 20-foot clear spans, exposed second-floor beams, porch posts and plates, rough window and door frames, spikes, and exterior caulk. Options include interior caulk, steel-threaded rod for wall connections, and box window frames, Also, 7- and 8-inch-diameter logs are available.

MATERIALS

Air-Lock logs are cut from ponderosa pine, drilled, then machined to an even diameter, which presents round log faces inside and out. Traditional Swedish cope construction (a concave saucer shape is milled into the bottom edge of each log) is combined with a single tongue and groove (t&g) locking system.

SPECIAL FEATURES

The Air-Lock log is unique. The firm has been making it for over fifty years. It minimizes some of the common problems with solid-log walls, such as shrinkage, twisting, and warping.

RELATIVE SIZE/COST

Air-Lock makes log packages costing from about $7,000 to $40,000. A representative log package with 1,240 square feet on the first floor and 666 square feet of loft space, totaling 1,906 square feet, is roughly $29,000; $15 per square foot.

COMPANY INFORMATION

Air-Lock ships to the western states, and estimates trucking costs at $2 per mile. The firm offers complete engineering and planning services and contracts for log home building in New Mexico. Their brochures are sent on request, a complete plan book is available for $5.

ALTA INDUSTRIES, LTD.

Box 88
Halcottsville, NY 12438
(914) 586-3336

PRODUCT RANGE

Alta offers thirty-five standard log home plans, both traditional and contemporary designs, ranging from small, 24-square-foot cabins to large homes of over 3,000 square feet.

PREFAB COMPONENTS

Alta standard log packages include precut double tongue and groove wall logs, log gable and roof rafters, posts and lintels for posts, laminated ceiling and ridge beams, second-floor decking, windows and exterior doors, plus spikes, caulk, and sealant—a complete log shell.

MATERIALS

Solid pine logs are used in walls. Loft and second-floor decking is 1⅛-inch plywood with t&g locking or 2-inch solid wood decking. Exterior windows are double-glazed, and exterior doors are metal-clad and foam-filled.

SPECIAL FEATURES

Alta has built homes and several commercial buildings in the eastern United States, including a 5,000-square-foot store in North Carolina. The firm allows a great degree of plan modification, including wall height, at little or no cost.

RELATIVE SIZE/COST

Alta's Altan III model with 936 square feet and 14 log courses is about $15,000; $16 per square foot. The large Glenford model with three bedrooms and garage and 3,116 square feet is about $32,000; $10 per square foot.

COMPANY INFORMATION

Alta will send a small color brochure on request; an information kit that costs $5 has all floor plans and renderings of the thirty-five models, plus a thorough report on log-wall mass gain thermal efficiency and construction details. The firm is a member of the National Association of Home Manufacturers and the Log Homes Council.

AMERICAN LINCOLN HOMES

P.O. Box 669
Battleboro, NC 27809
(800) 334-5166
(800) 682-8127 (in North
Carolina)

PRODUCT RANGE
American Lincoln offers fifty stock plans, including log homes in traditional and contemporary styles, ranging from 550- and 750-square-foot basic cabins to 2,500-square-foot homes. The company has also produced the first multiunit solid-log-wall condominiums (pictured). This innovation marks yet another milestone in the resurgence of log building, which has moved from small cabins to elaborate homes to commercial buildings, and now even apartments.

PREFAB COMPONENTS
Standard packages are available with two types of log wall. American Lincoln's Classic Log is gently rounded outside, machined top and bottom with double tongue and groove locking, and milled flat on the inside face with V-notch seams. Their Contemporary Beveled Log is altered on the outside to present a beveled, clapboard-type face. Full, 8-inch-thick walls with overlapped corners rest on pressure-treated sills. T&g log siding is used over trusses at gable ends. The precut package includes window and door bucks, prefab roof trusses with sheathing, ridge cap, felt paper, asphalt shingles, all windows and doors (with locksets), and all sealants, caulk, and spikes—creating a closed-in shell.

MATERIALS
Solid logs (enough for 7-foot-9-inch eave walls) are cut from white pine, with options for cypress and cedar. Roof trusses are decked with 5/8-inch CDX plywood. Windows are double-glazed and prehung, with screens and snap-in grilles. Exterior doors are 1¾-inch metal-clad, and foam-filled-in wood frames with locksets. The log walls are sealed with a ¼-inch bead of acrylic caulk on the double t&g joints, with keyed splines sealing seams at traditional butt-and-pass corners.

SPECIAL FEATURES
American Lincoln makes an intelligent effort to involve owners in the building process. They offer design help with plan modifications, and the best type of construction guide, with text, drawings, and valuable how-to photos. The firm goes one step further and offers audiovisual instruction. They are the first company in the industry to do so, although this practice makes so much sense that it will no doubt proliferate.

RELATIVE SIZE/COST
American Lincoln's small Pathfinder cabin with 748 square feet costs roughly $13,000 with white pine logs, $17,000 in cedar; $17 and $22 per square foot respectively. One of the larger models, the Montana, with 2,243 square feet, is approximately $27,000 in white pine and $36,000 in cedar; $12 and $16 per square foot respectively.

COMPANY INFORMATION
A color brochure with detailed illustrations of a typical model is sent on request. The firm's eighty-page color planning book with renderings and floor plans of all models, plus details on design and construction is $9.95.

APPALACHIAN LOG STRUCTURES

P.O. Box 86
Goshen, VA 24439
(304) 372-2211

PRODUCT RANGE

Appalachian is an interesting company offering forty standard models of log homes in seven styles: gambrel, ranch, loft, two-story, vacation, commercial, and custom. The Virginia-based firm produces distinctively southern varieties of log buildings, specifically flat-faced, hewn-log walls. Plans range from a 576-square-foot garage to a 4,960-square-foot condominium package. Nearly 80 percent of the homes sold are customized from stock plans.

PREFAB COMPONENTS

Three log styles are offered. Appalachian Round are t&g-joined in 6- or 8-inch diameters with a gently rounded exterior face and flat, V-jointed interior seams. Shadowlog is a unique beveled shape, also 6 or 8 inches thick with t&g joints, that creates a clapboard effect. Appalachian's Mountaineer Dovetail log is a classic 6 x 10-inch timber with dovetail corners and chinked seams. The firm does rough-saw the logs, but can finish them with a hand hewing to closely resemble fully hand-hewn beams. Log packages are all pre-cut and pressure-treated, also pre-drilled for spikes. (The firm even sends a spare bit for extra spike holes you may need to make.) All structural beams are included, rough-sawn and pressure-treated, plus windows and doors, anchors, sealers, and hardware, plus three sets of blueprints.

MATERIALS

Southern yellow pine is standard, with optional white pine or even oak. All logs are pressure-treated using the CCA waterborne salt system. Untreated timbers are available, although Appalachian covers treated wood with a twenty-five-year warranty against insect infestation and decay. Kits include Andersen Perma-Shield Narroline double-glazed windows with screens and snap-in grilles and Morgan prehung doors.

SPECIAL FEATURES

Appalachian sill logs are channeled so that electrical lines can be concealed around the perimeter, to avoid a problem found in some log homes. Another nice touch is pre-cut and routed 4 x 6-inch jambs to fit window openings that allow for wall settling.

RELATIVE SIZE/COST

The Conservator, a 960-square-foot home, is about $11,500 in flat-hewn logs, $12,500 in 6-inch round logs, and $14,000 in 8-inch round logs; $12, $13, and $15 per square foot respectively. The West Wind, a 3,296-square-foot model, is about $35,000 in hewn log, $43,000 in 6-inch round log, and $50,000 in 8-inch round log; $11, $13, and $15 respectively.

COMPANY INFORMATION

A portfolio including all floor plans and several color photos of each home (you wind up with a really good sense of the house) is sent for $6. A basic flier showing a few homes and the different log types is sent on request. Appalachian is a member of the North American Log Builders Association and the American Wood-Preservers Association.

AUTHENTIC HOMES CORP.

Box 1288
Laramie, WY 82070
(307) 742-3786

PRODUCT RANGE

Authentic produces over forty log home designs, traditional styles ranging from 400 and 500 square feet to several models with over 2,500 square feet. Two thirds of Authentic's homes are customized from stock plans.

PREFAB COMPONENTS

Kits contain all log components precut and marked for assembly, plus fasteners. Logs are 8- to 9-inch diameters peeled to leave natural round faces inside and out. Logs are flat-sawn top and bottom at 6-inch depths. Spline keys are used to connect butt-end logs in the wall. Construction adhesive and 10-inch spikes pin the wall logs together through predrilled holes.

MATERIALS

Authentic uses seasoned heartwood (from the middle of the tree), western pine species, with less than 15 percent moisture content to minimize shrinkage and disruption at frame openings. More complete kits with precut dimensional timber can be purchased, although standard kits include wall logs, gable ends, log rafters for cathedral ceilings, beams and joists for exposed second-floor frames, plus log stairs and balconies.

SPECIAL FEATURES

Authentic's log walls are easy to assemble. Logs are simply stacked one on another over adhesive and spikes, forming butt-and-pass corners (an alternative-weave pattern, where one log runs on top of and past the previous course). Authentic also provides two types of logs: the Rustic Profile, a debarked full-round log, and the Contemporary Profile, with a shallow round outside, and uniform rounded or flat face inside.

RELATIVE SIZE/COST

The 858-square-foot Bridger model log package is roughly $7,500 with Profile logs, $9,500 with Rustic logs; $9 and $11 per square foot respectively. The Iroquois, one of the company's largest models at 2,842 square feet, is roughly $23,000 with the machined logs and $26,500 with Rustic logs; $8 and $9 respectively—low, even for the log-only packages.

COMPANY INFORMATION

Authentic sends a full-color plan catalog book for $6, and basic information on request. They also have two interesting booklets worth writing for: one on the general characteristics and performance of wood and different wood species, and one on planning, with a realistic look at financing, codes, and an unusual, detailed breakdown of the time required for step-by-step assembly.

BEAVER LOG HOMES
P.O. Box 1145
Claremore, OK 74017
(918) 341-5932

PRODUCT RANGE
Beaver Log produces close to fifty stock plans, but can fabricate precut log kits for any size home. The smallest cabin is 572 square feet, and they have built homes over 4,000 square feet. Traditional cabin designs predominate, although there are a few unorthodox models with mansard and half-hip roofs.

PREFAB COMPONENTS
Beaver Log makes precut kits with 8-, 10-, and 12-inch-diameter logs, joined after milling to uniform diameters with a double tongue and groove locking system. The shell package includes all wall logs, caulking, gaskets, and preservative.

MATERIALS
Beaver Log makes a turned pine log, meaning that the visible log faces are rounded and uniform, while double t&g surfaces are milled top and bottom. Log ends at precut openings are channeled for the use of a spline system at windows and doors. Precutting also allows predrilling, and Beaver Log takes advantage of log alignment by using full-height, through-the-wall steel bolts. In a hurricane, all the house walls would have to blow away in one piece.

SPECIAL FEATURES
Beaver Log walls are engineered, but you can't tell unless you look closely. Even though tongue and groove seams are visible at log ends on overlapped corners, the company precuts traditional saddle notches, a detail common to handcrafted log homes but not often found on precut kits easily assembled by owner-builders.

RELATIVE SIZE/COST
Costs are quoted on request. But Bill Sitler from Beaver Log writes, "Last year we had one built for $23 per square foot, another came in at $78." The company's most popular model (pictured) is the Broken Arrow, a 1,219-square-foot layout with loft from which hundreds of plans have been generated with minor alterations. Over three quarters of all Beaver Log homes are customized by owners from stock plans.

COMPANY INFORMATION
Working from six mills (Oklahoma, Alaska, Washington, Texas, Nebraska, Michigan), the firm uses locally available species of pine: southern yellow or ponderosa or lodgepole, for example. Complete plan books are available for $5. Basic literature and a sample of the company's monthly newsletter are sent on request. Beaver Log is a member of the Log Homes Council and the North American Log Builders Association.

GASTINEAU LOG HOMES

Highway 54
New Bloomfield, MO
65063
(314) 896-5611

PRODUCT RANGE

Gastineau offers thirty stock plans, ranging from approximately 400 to 3,200 square feet. Styles range from a one-room trail cabin just over 400 square feet to two-story western-style homes, mansard roofs, and more. In addition, the company builds to specifications, and offers a custom-blueprint service. Interestingly, these design services are priced by the square foot (20 cents per square foot of designed space).

PREFAB COMPONENTS

Two types of packages are available: a basic, log-sealer kit, including all logs, caulking, spikes, butyl gaskets, etc.; and a full kit, including basic frame, partition walls, subflooring, structural and finished roofing, windows and doors—the works.

MATERIALS

Gastineau's president, Lynn Gastineau Repper, writes, "We have the distinction of being the only company in the United States to offer oak, pine, and walnut log homes. Our biggest seller is the oak, because of its durability and aesthetic appeal. Plus it is the same price as the pine!" All logs are cut from 12- to 15-inch-diameter trees and air-dried for six months. The finished logs are uniform in size, 7½ inches wide, and joined with a double tongue and groove. Flat or round interior surfaces may be selected according to taste.

SPECIAL FEATURES

Gastineau offers wood-frame, thermal-pane, prehung windows with screens (a choice of Andersen Terratone or Weathervane). CCA-treated timbers are used for sill plates, floor joists, and girders, with planed oak for beams, posts, and flooring. Full blueprints are included in the complete kit, and minor changes to standard plans will be made at no cost. Kits do not include labor, foundation, insu-

lation, or mechanical systems, all of which is made plain in the company's literature.

RELATIVE SIZE/COST

Gastineau's largest stock plan (3,128 square feet) costs roughly $40,000 for a full-basement, full-kit package; $12.00 per square foot. The same model as a log-sealer kit for slab costs roughly $14,000; $4.30 per square foot. A small, 840-square-foot cabin costs roughly $18,000 for a full-basement, full-kit package; $18.00 per square foot. The same cabin as a log-sealer kit for slab costs roughly $7,000; $7.80 per square foot.

COMPANY INFORMATION

The company offers a small color booklet plus a plan guide with an illustration and detailed floor plan of every standard model for $5. Standard blueprints can be purchased for $25. Gastineau Log Homes is a charter member of the North American Log Builders Association. (Lynn Repper serves as their president for 1985.) Also, the firm belongs to the National Home Builders Association.

GREATWOOD LOG HOMES, INC.

P.O. Box 707
Elkhart Lake, WI 53020
(800) 558-5812
(800) 242-1021
(in Wisconsin)

PRODUCT RANGE

Greatwood now offers close to a hundred different stock plans for log homes, ranging from small cabins to large, multistory designs, plus some slightly odd, swept-wing contemporary designs that seem to be fighting the hand-peeled logs overlapping at corners. In any case, there is an incredible variety, in full- and face-log construction, with solar envelopes, gambrel roofs—you name it.

PREFAB COMPONENTS

Hand-peeled log walls and all structural log members, such as porch posts and rafters, are pre-cut. The Full-Log package provides logs milled on top and bottom with V-notched corners, and full-thickness log overlaps. Logs are pinned with spikes and ¾-inch steel rod at intervals.

MATERIALS

Greatwood offers a choice of cedar or pine logs, all hand-peeled. Double gaskets are used between logs for weather sealing, with wood-tone caulk at corners. Full logs are used on exposed porch rafters and roof log trusses, while concealed framing is 2 x 10 floor joists under ⅝-inch plywood subflooring. Windows are triple-glazed.

SPECIAL FEATURES

For those who are not convinced about the mass gain energy effect of solid log walls, Greatwood offers a combination of log and conventional stick building called Ultra Log. Smoothly surfaced, distinctively hand-finished (you can see the marks of the drawshave) logs are full width at corners, but only half thick along the wall length. Here they are backed by a fully insulated 2 x 6 studwall and one inch of Styrofoam sheathing for a minimum R-30 cold-climate rating. Ultra Log kits provide R-40 in the roof.

RELATIVE SIZE/COST

Specific costs for Greatwood homes are quoted on request. The company's smallest cabins cost about $10,000.

COMPANY INFORMATION

Greatwood provides a complete planning guide for $7, and information packages on their specialized solar-envelope models. The firm offers design help, and will prepare working plans so that owner-builders can obtain permits. Greatwood is a member of the North American Log Builders Association.

GREEN MOUNTAIN LOG HOMES
Box 190
Chester, VT 05143
(802) 875-2163

PRODUCT RANGE
Green Mountain makes a large number of stock-plan log homes, large and small, both traditional and modern, including passive solar buildings. Their color brochure features a knockout called the Sugar House, a beautiful combination of horizontal and vertical log walls with a raised roof area over the main room creating a clerestory.

PREFAB COMPONENTS
Typical log packages include hand-peeled logs for 8-foot-high walls, spikes, 9-inch-diameter crosstie beams, triple-glazed double-hung windows, and pine-plank exterior doors. The firm also groups packages of finishing items such as tongue and groove decking, and packages of shell items such as dimensional timbers for roof and floor framing. Green Mountain stresses design flexibility.

MATERIALS
Log walls are hand-peeled spruce, producing an R-value of about 12, although the company correctly notes that a more realistic figure is R-14 to R-18, considering the mass gain effect of solid timber walls.

SPECIAL FEATURES
The hand-peeled logs are irregular, and joined at corners with traditional saddle notches. This method produces a handcrafted effect, even though the concealed surfaces of the logs are machined flat. Seams between logs are sealed by inserting the firm's proprietary spline system, called Arrowspline, into a central groove. The vinyl spline is shaped like a stack of arrowheads, which compress slightly as a log is set down in place, then exert pressure against the sides of the groove, preventing withdrawal, and air and water infiltration.

RELATIVE SIZE/COST
Green Mountain offers a small vacation cabin their literature describes forthrightly as "frankly skinned down for a truly small vacation home" for roughly $9,000. The 16 x 24-foot log package runs roughly $23 per square foot. The Grafton model, a two-story main cabin (with a Colonial touch where the second floor overhangs the first) plus an ell, with 2,300 square feet, is roughly $50,000; $21 per square foot.

COMPANY INFORMATION
Green Mountain provides outstanding consumer literature. Rarely will you see such plain-language, no-nonsense brochures that anticipate consumer questions. The company also offers, for $4.50, a package of information titled "Designing Your Own Green Mountain Log Home." It includes elevation views, different rafter angles, different wall sections, even furniture, all on preprinted sheets. Instructions help you to put together a floor plan, then select needed components and timbers, then price each item. Another booklet, a bit overpriced at $8, offers thirty-seven construction drawings and thirteen pages of text on log home building. Start by requesting Green Mountain's small color brochure. Where many firms conjure up consumer questions such as "How soon can I get delivery of my beautiful new XYZ log home?" Green Mountain includes disarmingly real questions such as "What is the cheapest model you have?" Hats off to a company that keeps their potential customers in mind, and not the hyped-up image of their products. Green Mountain is a charter member of the Log Homes Council.

GREEN RIVER TRADING CO.

Millerton, NY 12546
(518) 789-3311

PRODUCT RANGE

Green River offers eight basic log home plans, ranging from 748 to 2,761 square feet in three types of construction: a double tongue and groove 6½ x 7-inch log with two round faces, a 6½ x 6-inch log with rounded exterior and flat-faced interior, and a 1¼ x 6-inch log facing shiplap siding to cover conventional studding. Green River also builds garages, barns, custom designs, and other commercial log structures.

PREFAB COMPONENTS

Green River packages include all full wall logs, exposed roof beams on some designs, porch posts and plates, polyethylene gasket sealers, spikes, acrylic caulk, clear wood preservative for exterior on-site application, and four sets of construction blueprints.

MATERIALS

Green River builds with milled white pine logs with interlocking, V-type, double tongue and groove seams. Walls are constructed with traditional butt-and-pass corners. Flat interior surfaces present a tight, knotty pine wall.

SPECIAL FEATURES

Green River estimates a typical job as follows: delivery within thirty days of ordering, one week to erect the log frame. All but their largest models arrive on a single flatbed truck.

RELATIVE SIZE/COST

The smallest Green River home, the Ranch I with 748 square feet, is roughly $9,000; $12 per square foot. One of the largest models, the Solar Saltbox with 2,761 square feet, is roughly $21,000; $8 per square foot. Special-order logs include 7-inch widths (15 percent additional), 8-inch widths (25 percent more), and other sizes up to large, 10-inch widths that increase the package price by 45 percent.

COMPANY INFORMATION

Green River sends a small flier on request, and their full plan book for $5. Green River is a charter member of the North American Log Builders Association.

HERITAGE LOG HOMES

P.O. Box 610
Gatlinburg, TN 37738
(800) 251-0973
(615) 436-9331
(in Tennessee)

PRODUCT RANGE
Heritage makes thirty log homes, three freestanding log garages, and precut custom designs. The homes are traditional log designs, ranging from a two-bedroom cabin with 861 square feet to an immense five-bedroom, three-and-a-half-bath log home of 4,877 square feet.

PREFAB COMPONENTS
Heritage Basic Shell kits include all precut and numbered log walls (all window and door openings are accounted for, eliminating waste); 6/6-light double-hung, double-glazed windows; solid-core 9-light crossbuck exterior doors; all posts, girders, collar ties, and ridge beam; gaskets and sealants; 10-inch spikes; assembly manual; and three full sets of working drawings. The "Dry-In" shell includes 4 x 8-foot insulated panels (either R-20 or R-30). The interior panel faces have a grooved plywood skin to simulate t&g decking.

MATERIALS
Select pine logs are milled to 8-inch diameters with round faces inside and out, with double tongue and groove for locking and weatherizing. Foam strips seal each tongue along the log, with foam gaskets sealing saddle-notch corners. The logs are debarked, air-dried, and treated with preservative (currently the EPA-approved Mitrol PQ-57).

SPECIAL FEATURES
Round log faces and traditional saddle-notch corners give Heritage homes as much of a handcrafted appearance as is possible with milled t&g logs. The only giveaway is double t&g patterns on the end grain of overlapped corner logs outside the house. Heritage sells complete blueprints for $30 ($25 for three copies, commonly required for permits and estimates). Costs are rebated from the log home purchase if you decide to order.

RELATIVE SIZE/COST
Two-bed, one-bath Woodland models with 1,085 square feet are roughly $15,000 for log-shell packages ($13.50 per square foot), roughly $19,000, including insulated roof panels ($17 per square foot). A larger, four-bedroom, two-bath Cedaridge model with 2,125 square feet is roughly $18,000 for the basic shell ($8 per square foot), roughly $22,000 with insulated panels ($10 per square foot).

COMPANY INFORMATION
A color brochure is sent on request. The forty-eight-page color plan book with details on construction, energy efficiency, costs, and pictorial and plan views of all models costs $6. Heritage is a member of the Log Homes Council.

HERITAGE SOLID WOOD HOMES

Route 9, Box 37
Idaho Falls, ID 83401
(208) 529-5659

PRODUCT RANGE
Heritage precuts solid log wall homes ranging from 436 square feet to just over 2,000 square feet, presenting fifteen standard plans and two series of more contemporary, passive solar designs.

PREFAB COMPONENTS
Standard Heritage packages include all exterior 6 x 6 log walls, interior 4 x 6 bearing walls, solid-core exterior doors, wood frame double-glazed windows, log beams for exposed second-floor framing, and roof beams. Additional items to make a more complete package include 2 x 6 t&g decking for floors and roofs, all precut and labeled.

MATERIALS
The Heritage log is cut from standing dead lodgepole pine. Butt seams in the wall are eliminated with a double tongue and groove locking system. A groove and spline system seals horizontal seams between the machined logs. The precut logs are cut with a "Lincoln Log" square saddle notch, which resembles a traditional, curved seam saddle notch when assembled. A gentle curve on exterior faces is backed with a double tongue and groove weather joint in addition to the spline seal, plus spikes and gaskets.

SPECIAL FEATURES
Heritage is one of the few companies that handles the product from the first phases of timber selection and logging through transportation, precutting, and in-house transport to the building site.

RELATIVE SIZE/COST
The Tyrolian model with 717 square feet and two bedrooms is approximately $11,500; $16 per square foot. One of the larger, two-story, more contemporary models, the Regional, with 2,010 square feet, is approximately $30,000; $15 per square foot.

COMPANY INFORMATION
Heritage provides a brief color flier with several photos and details of the log construction on request. Their plan package, consisting of fifteen designs with renderings, is sent for $5.

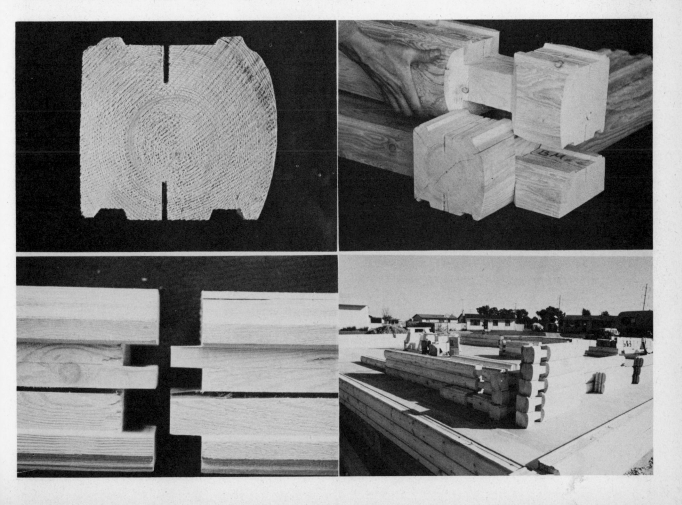

LOG STRUCTURES OF THE SOUTH

Port of Sanford,
P.O. Box 276
Lake Monroe, FL 32747
(305) 831-5028

PRODUCT RANGE

Log Structures offers over twenty different stock plans, from single-room cabins to four-bedroom homes, and customized design. The log homes are available in traditional cabin styles, and more modern styles with steep, broken-back rafters, sliding glass doors, and large fixed-glass panels.

PREFAB COMPONENTS

Complete shells are available.

MATERIALS

Log Structures uses eastern white pine, red cypress, and western red cedar. The logs are milled to show flat sides inside and out, the modern equivalent of flat-sided, hand-hewn timbers, used more in the South than full-round log walls, which predominate in the North-east. All wall timbers are milled 5 inches thick.

SPECIAL FEATURES

Many prefab log home companies mill logs into uniform sizes with some form of tongue and groove locking pattern. Log Structures of the South cuts in a double tongue and groove with one interesting addition. On the exterior face of the log (left slightly rounded) a mini-water table the firm calls its "drip-lip" design is cut into outside edges, keeping wind-driven rain out of the log joints.

RELATIVE SIZE/COST

Quoted on inquiry.

COMPANY INFORMATION

The firm offers a "Home Planning Portfolio" for $4. A one-page color flier is sent on request.

NEW ENGLAND LOG HOMES, INC.

P.O. Box 5056
2301 State Street
Hamden, CT 06518
(203) 562-9981

PRODUCT RANGE

New England Log has over forty plans for hand-peeled log homes, from a small cabin at 252 square feet called the Thoreau, to the Timberwood model at 3,328 square feet, all available with many customized options.

PREFAB COMPONENTS

The firm provides two different types of log home kits. Their Total Log Package includes precut 7- to 11-inch-diameter t&g wall logs, plates, sills, joists, collar ties, roof trusses, timber rafters, dormer logs, all sealants and sealing splines, precut window casings, prehung windows and doors, t&g decking, and finished roofing. Their Basic Log Package excludes decking, insulation, and roofing.

MATERIALS

New England Log's hand-peeled, select logs present a unique mottled effect. All are dip-treated in a EPA-approved (registered) pre-servative, and arrive at the site already treated by the Orkin Exterminating Company. Three log types are available: a single t&g peeled log with rounded interior and exterior faces, the Duolog with rounded and peeled exterior but square-sawn interior, and the Panellog, machined on four sides, with a slightly rounded exterior face.

SPECIAL FEATURES

New England Log Homes are certified free of powder-post beetles and borers, and backed by a pest-free warranty for one year. Precut log packages and a detailed "Construction Guide" with step-by-step photographs allow inexperienced owner-builders to erect a small log home in only five or six days. A crew can finish the company's largest model in twenty-one days.

RELATIVE SIZE/COST

New England Log packages range from about $7,500 to $60,000. The small, 252-square-foot Thoreau cabin is roughly $8,500 for the basic log package, $9,500 for the total log kit; $33 and $38 per square foot respectively. The 3,328-square-foot Timberwood model is roughly $44,000 for the basic log package, and $58,000 for the total package; $13 and $17 per square foot respectively.

COMPANY INFORMATION

New England Log Homes works through a network of over a hundred franchised dealers across the U.S. and Canada, with regional manufacturing plants in Massachusetts, Virginia, Missouri, and California, which reduces shipping costs and delivery time of customized models. Basic information is sent on request. A full-color planning kit is $6. The firm is a member of the National Association of Home Builders.

NORTHERN PRODUCTS LOG HOMES, INC.

P.O. Box 616
Bomarc Road
Bangor, ME 04401
(207) 945-6413

PRODUCT RANGE

Northern Products makes a wide range of almost customized log homes—*almost* because they do offer a range of what they call "starter plans," but encourage customers to make changes and add the details best suited to their needs. Traditional log home designs are precut from pine logs, and machined to form a gently rounded exterior face with a flat interior face.

PREFAB COMPONENTS

Northern Products log packages include precut and numbered logs matched to blueprint layouts, with precut openings, spikes, roofing, partitions, flooring, triple-glazed windows, and two-layer roof insulation.

MATERIALS

The company precuts 6 x 8 eastern white pine logs, leaving a wide tongue and groove top and bottom for alignment and sealing seams against the weather. This joint is reinforced with an oil-based caulk and a foam gasket.

SPECIAL FEATURES

One of the most interesting features of this firm is their program of reforestation. Normally, planting new seedlings to replace harvested trees is the responsibility of lumber companies. But Northern Products has instituted a program of planting a seedling for every log used in every log home they sell. They deserve credit for coming up with a plan that practices what many others only preach.

RELATIVE SIZE/COST

Because Northern Products' starter plans are customized to a great degree, quotes will be given on request for specific floor plans.

COMPANY INFORMATION

Northern Products has thorough information on mass gain and energy calculations on log walls, including a synopsis of the interesting test conducted by the National Bureau of Standards comparing log walls to various conventional types of construction. Their complete plans catalog is sent for $6.

ROCKY MOUNTAIN LOG HOMES

3353 Highway 93 South
Hamilton, MT 59840
(406) 363-5680

PRODUCT RANGE

Rocky Mountain offers thirty-four standard plans, ranging from a 440-square-foot cabin to 5,000-square-foot homes, also active and passive solar designs, and commercial log buildings such as restaurants, churches, and buildings for the U.S. Forest Service. Although all models are built with machined logs, the Swedish cope construction (a dish-shaped cutout that lets wall logs nestle together) and the quality of traditional saddle joints at corners make these homes as close to handcrafted as you can get.

PREFAB COMPONENTS

Rocky Mountain homes are precut and prenotched from dry-standing timber. Solid log walls are available in seven sizes, from 7- to 12-inch diameters, and a unique, special-order, massive 18-inch diameter—the largest manufactured log available to consumers. Complete packages include all structural logs, rafters, tie beams, and such. The firm can also provide t&g decking materials, all windows and doors, even complete mechanical packages.

MATERIALS

Rocky Mountain logs are cut from dry stands of cedar, white pine, and ponderosa pine. The full-round logs provide a structural and naturally insulated wall, finished inside and out.

SPECIAL FEATURES

The overriding feature of Rocky Mountain homes is summed up by company president Jim Schueler, who writes, "We build no gimmicks into Rocky Mountain Log Homes." You get big logs, without splines or tongue and groove systems—just massive timbers that look quite different from the highly machined products of most log kit companies.

RELATIVE SIZE/COST

Because of the tremendous variation in home size (440 to over 5,000 square feet) and the variation in possible kit components, you should write or call for quotes

on specific models. To give you an idea, though, a small 7-inch-diameter log package costing roughly $9,000 will increase to roughly $10,000 built with 12-inch logs. Rocky Mountain sells basic packages priced from $5,000 to $100,000.

COMPANY INFORMATION

Rocky Mountain ships six hundred homes annually, including sixty to Alaska last year, many to Vermont, and even to Florida. The firm's large, full-color plan book with floor plans and views of all models, and a stunning collection of inte-

rior and exterior pictures of their log homes, costs $6. A brief color brochure is sent on request. Their "Construction Manual" (for owner-builders or contractors) is carefully detailed, with understandable drawings and a practical text.

SOUTHERN CYPRESS LOG HOMES, INC.

P.O. Box 209
Crystal River, FL 32629
(904) 795-0777

PRODUCT RANGE

Southern Cypress offers twenty-two stock plans ranging from roughly 500 to over 3,000 square feet, all in traditional log home styles. Although the firm can supply yellow pine log frames, they also offer all models in tidewater heart cypress and western red cedar.

PREFAB COMPONENTS

Southern Cypress builds homes with two types of corner details: the butt and pass overlap, and their more popular version, a European dovetail notch. Log walls can be selected in three different materials and four patterns: a 6 x 8 log with gently rounded exterior face and flat-sawn, V-jointed interior; a 6 x 6 log in the same pattern; a 6 x 8 log with hand-hewn exterior face; and a 6 x 8 log with smooth-sawn and beveled exterior. Standard kits include all double tongue and groove logs, caulk, splines, spiral shank spikes, blueprints, and four hours of on-site assistance.

MATERIALS

The firm's unusual offering, tidewater cypress *(Taxodium distichum)*, is a deep-swamp growth found in the coastal plains of the southeastern states. It is darker, more finely textured, more durable, and contains less sapwood than the readily available inland growth classified as yellow cypress. The wood contains an oil that is highly antiseptic, and toxic in preventing the development of fungi that cause decay. The U.S. Bureau of Entomology has found tidewater cypress immune to termite attack even when adjoining timbers of other wood species were completely infested.

SPECIAL FEATURES

Cypress shingles on Mount Vernon are in good condition after 250 years. That's one of many testimonials to the exceptional durability of cypress, pointing up its resistance to decay, wood disease, and insects. Also, it does not require chemical pressure-treating.

RELATIVE SIZE/COST

Southern Cypress's Appalachian model (pictured), with 1,424 square feet of living space and 248 square feet of garage, porch, and storage space, is roughly $8,000 in 6 x 6 yellow pine, and $9,000 in either 6 x 6 or 6 x 8 tidewater heart cypress. The same model is about $10,000 in western red cedar; roughly $5 to $6 per square foot. Dovetail notch detailing adds about $600 to the total cost.

COMPANY INFORMATION

The firm provides a catalog of all models with basic renderings and floor plans for $4.95. The company will quote prices on custom designs.

SOUTHLAND LOG HOMES, INC.

Route 2, Box 5-B
Irmo, SC 29063
(803) 781-5100

PRODUCT RANGE

Southland offers ten different traditional designs for log homes, each available with seven different floor plans. Also, the firm allows nearly limitless customizing by merging basic styles, partition wall layouts, and planning for wing additions. Their planning guide contains thirty-four stock floor plans in ten styles, ranging from about 1,300 to 3,000 square feet.

PREFAB COMPONENTS

Southland builds log home packages using kiln-dried (kd) timbers. Standard kits include all 8 x 6 kd, precut log walls, log floor joists between first and second floors, log post and lintels, shiplap log siding for gable ends and dormers, all windows and exterior doors, spikes, adhesive, Aquatrol wood finish/sealer, caulk, building plans and start-up supervision.

MATERIALS

Southland can provide walls with two round faces, with a round exterior and flat interior, and two beveled patterns, all cut from southern yellow pine, all kiln-dried. Typical corners are traditional butt-and-pass, with 45-degree miters or bevel log models.

SPECIAL FEATURES

Southland provides exceptionally stable and well-protected logs, combining kiln-dried pine, chemical pressure treating at the factory (the logs are dipped in wood preservative and insecticide), and preservative finish coating on site.

RELATIVE SIZE/COST

Southland's Richmond model with 1,716 square feet plus over 400 square feet of porch space is $19,000, about $11 per square foot. One of the largest models, with 3,948 square feet of living space, is roughly $41,000; $10 per square foot.

COMPANY INFORMATION

Southland provides a color planning guide showing the basic styles and alternative floor plans for each, for $6. The firm ships nationally and is a charter member of the North American Log Builders Association.

WILDERNESS LOG HOMES, INC.
RR 2
Plymouth, WI 53073
(800) BEST-LOG
(800) 852-LOGS
(in Wisconsin)

PRODUCT RANGE
Wilderness Log makes forty different traditional log homes, offering full logs machined top and bottom for flat bearing and a tight weather seal with two strips of urethane sealer, and what the company calls Insulog, a half-log system applied over a conventional, insulated studwall. This design maintains the full-log exterior appearance (full-width logs are left exposed at overlapped corners), but amounts to an overbuilt wall: logs and a 2 x 6 dimensional frame.

PREFAB COMPONENTS
The Wilderness full-round log package includes wall logs with mitered corner joints, backer rod sealers, spikes, double-hung, double-glazed windows and frames and doors, all partition materials, all roofing materials, plus joists, bridging, and materials for second-floor frames. An extensive list of options includes knotty pine paneling, oversize handcrafted log rafters, and complete floor systems.

MATERIALS
The firm uses 10-inch-diameter cedar and pine logs on full-log walls. The Wilderness half-log system combines these half timbers with 2 x 6 studs, 1-inch Tuff-R sheathing, a vapor barrier, and full-depth fiber glass insulation. Standard materials include 1¾-inch, 9-light crossbuck exterior doors, ⅝-inch roof deck with 260 fiber glass shingles, knotty pine soffits, with options for hand-split roof shakes, dormers, and ridge vents.

SPECIAL FEATURES
The Wilderness corner system is built on simple V-notch mortises, easily assembled and spiked by owner-builders.

RELATIVE SIZE/COST
The Homesteader, a 370-square-foot cabin with covered porch, costs roughly $26,000 for the complete full-log package; $70 per square foot. The Williamsburg, a large, two-story 1,488-square-foot log home with three bedrooms and two baths on the second floor of the main wing, costs roughly $47,000; $31 per square foot.

COMPANY INFORMATION
Wilderness Log Homes sells through more than a hundred dealerships across the United States, and one in Japan. If they can ship across the Pacific they can probably locate your building site, too. Basic information is sent on request; a complete planning guide with floor plans and illustrations of all models is $6. The firm is a member of the Log Homes Council.

POST AND BEAM HOMES

AMERICAN TIMBER HOMES, INC.

Escanaba, MI 49829
(906) 786-4550

PRODUCT RANGE

This firm could also be listed under manufactured homes. They make panelized cedar houses built around heavy timber frames with exposed dimensional timber or full-log roof trusses. A wide selection is offered in three categories: traditional cabins and chalets, clean-lined contemporary cedarwall homes, and similar styles adapted for solar efficiency, all ranging from about 600 to 3,600 square feet.

PREFAB COMPONENTS

American Timber supplies two types of packages. Their closed shell includes exterior panelized walls with 2 x 6 framing, ½-inch sheathing, insulation, felt paper, and exterior siding; windows and doors; panelized roofing over hand-peeled log trusses or dimensional timbers with a 2-inch deck, 3-inch rigid foam insulating board, and ½-inch plywood plus trim, felt, and fiber glass shingles; first- and second-story floor frames and ¾-inch underlayment, interior partitions, and porch frames with a 2-inch cedar deck. The firm's complete package also includes all interior finishing materials, such as interior doors, paneling, stairs, and trim.

MATERIALS

Panelized walls are ¾-inch rough-sawn vertical northern white cedar, preservative-sealed, with ¾-inch t&g planking inside available in several wood species, including ash, cherry, cedar, and aspen. Exposed log trusses are bolted sections of hand-peeled balsam fir. Exterior doors are metal-clad foam core, prehung with double glazing, and optional triple glazing. Double-glazed windows are wood-framed with vinyl cladding.

SPECIAL FEATURES

American Timber provides a unique combination of handcrafted custom construction and high-tech, panelized mass production. The interiors of the living rooms (called great rooms) on some models, with cedar over huge, clear-span log trusses framing a cathedral ceiling, just don't look like traditional manufactured housing.

RELATIVE SIZE/COST

The chalet design Vista Sportsman (pictured) with 768 square feet is about $27,000 for the closed-shell package and $30,000 for the complete package; $35 and $39 per square foot respectively. One of the large Country Squire models, with 1,568 square feet, is about $41,000 for the closed-shell package and $46,000 for the complete package; $26 and $29 per square foot respectively.

COMPANY INFORMATION

American Timber provides a full plan book with floor plans and views of their homes for $6. The firm sells anywhere east of the Rockies, delivering precut, panelized packages in their own trucks, accompanied by a factory-trained supervisor.

DECK HOUSE, INC.
930 Main Street
Acton, MA 01720
(617) 259-9450

PRODUCT RANGE
Deck House, in business since 1960, has developed a portfolio of fifty designs ranging from 1,500 to over 4,000 square feet. The firm stresses modification of their plans to suit individual needs. The designs are contemporary, with large clear-span areas, and high-quality cedar over post and beam frames.

PREFAB COMPONENTS
After a design is selected, Deck House ships a complete precut home shell for assembly on the owner-prepared foundation. The package includes pressure-treated sill, framing, windows, exterior and interior doors, insulation, siding, roofing, balcony and screened porch, interior partitions, stairs, and all trim.

MATERIALS
Deck House materials are uniformly first quality. The 2 x 4 wall studs are kiln-dried for exceptional stability, with ½-inch CDX sheathing. All double-glazed windows are mahogany-framed, and 4 x 12-inch and 4 x 14-inch Douglas fir beams

for floor and roof are decked with Red Cedar Potlatch Lock-Deck. Exterior doors are flush panel, solid-core mahogany. Siding is t&g Atlantic white cedar or western cedar. The list of materials occupies two pages of the Deck House catalog, staying with mahogany trim, kiln-dried studs, and treated sills on partition walls.

SPECIAL FEATURES
Deck House offers extensive planning and design help down to the fine points of cabinet arrangement in the kitchen, solar orientation, and options including Heat Mirror windows that have a chemically coated film seal between double glazing. With 0°F. outside temperatures, the inside surface of a conventional double-glazed window is roughly 43°. With Heat Mirror this improves to roughly 59°. This system has an R-value of 4.0, an improvement over triple glazing at R-2.6.

RELATIVE SIZE/COST
Deck House packages range between $40 and $50 per square foot

(less garage and basement areas) for most models. One of the smaller, 1,500-square-foot homes is about $30,000 for Deck House materials, an estimated $48,000 for construction; totaling $78,000, or $52 per square foot. One of the larger, 3,900-square-foot homes is about $60,000 for the Deck House package, $107,000 for construction; totaling $167,000, or $43 per square foot.

COMPANY INFORMATION
Deck House offers an elaborate presentation of several outsize, full-color, thorough, and detailed plan books for $12. The hefty package, covering every detail down to the drawer slides on kitchen cabinets, materials, options, and planning help, is free at the ten Deck House model home sites in the eastern United States, Illinois, Ohio, and Texas. Call (800) 225-5755 for information on the presentation or model sites. Deck House has shipped to every state except Alaska—over four thousand homes to date.

FOX-MAPLE POST & BEAM

P.O. Box 209
North Conway, NH 03860
(603) 356-2061

PRODUCT RANGE

Fox-Maple is still a small company, with a history typical of firms committed to a specific type of construction requiring hand skills and attention to detail. That may not sound like prefab building, and for Fox-Maple's first ten years it wasn't. They built custom timber frame homes. But they started a newsletter (heavy on company information, with solid articles on the craft as well), and the only mail-order tool catalog specifically slanted for timber framers. With that background, Fox-Maple recently introduced two classic frames as predesigned, precut packages: the saltbox (pictured) and a Cape, both of which can be adapted to different floor plans. The Saltbox is 28 x 36, with room for three or four bedrooms upstairs. The Cape is 26 x 36, with room for two small bedrooms and a bath upstairs.

PREFAB COMPONENTS

Both styles are cut from select native pine and offered as frame only or as frame with shell kits that include stress-skin insulating panels, roofing, and clapboards.

MATERIALS

Fox-Maple frames use pine and oak with traditional joinery common to New England homes built between 1720 and 1840—largely mortise and tenon joints with oak pegging. Frames may be ordered in pine with oak braces, or all in oak. Complete shell materials include R-30 wall panels, 235-pound asphalt shingles, #1 pine clapboard siding, and all nails and hardware. Owners usually supply their own foundation, utilities, interior finishing, and windows, although Fox-Maple will include them if requested.

SPECIAL FEATURES

The Saltbox shown could easily be seventeenth- or eighteenth-century. Interior exposed joinery is a treat in itself. These homes are like new antiques—a very positive juxtaposition of traditional design and construction methods in a brand-new, energy-efficient home.

RELATIVE SIZE/COST

The Saltbox frame is roughly $17,000 in pine and $22,000 in oak. The complete shell with optional assembly offered by Fox-Maple (they'll quote you a price) is roughly $37,000 in pine and $43,000 in oak. The Cape frame is about $14,000 in pine and $18,000 in oak; $30,000 for the complete shell in pine and $35,000 in oak. Frame prices begin at about $10 per square foot for usable living space, which totals 1,296 in the Cape.

COMPANY INFORMATION

Fox-Maple builds complete custom homes regionally, and will arrange to precut and erect a frame or complete shell, or simply ship the materials and blueprints to ambitious owner-builders or their contractors. A simple, elegant presentation of these two homes is worth writing for if classic Colonial lines appeal to you.

HABITAT AMERICAN BARN

123 Elm Street
South Deerfield, MA
01373
(413) 665-4006

PRODUCT RANGE

Habitat makes a wide variety of post and beam homes with exposed heavy timber framing. American Barn models range from a 1,168-square-foot model to two models (one classic Colonial and one modern adaptation of the basic Cape plan) of 2,352 square feet.

The Habitat series includes the Salem line, a group of homes that translate classic architectural lines and steeply sloped roof lines to current needs, including high energy efficiency and glazing walls. The firm offers roughly fifty stock plans.

PREFAB COMPONENTS

Precut American Barn packages include complete post and beam timber frame, prefabricated exterior wall system using kiln-dried 2 x 4s, t&g cedar or prestained kiln-dried pine siding plus 1-inch t&g Styrofoam insulation (additional in-wall batts are supplied by the owner), Tyvek Housewrap air infiltration barrier, all exterior trim, roof insulation and shingles, windows and doors, stairs, skylights, and all fasteners. The foundation, interior finishing, and mechanical systems are usually left to the owner.

MATERIALS

The firm uses western fir 8 x 8 posts, 3-inch-thick laminated t&g planking on loft floors and exposed roof deck, joining post and beam frames with mortise joints. Exposed rafters are 8 x 8 inches. Solid wood, heavy timber details include full 4-inch-thick stair tread planks. Exterior doors are wood frame with metal cladding and wood overlay, producing an R-14. Windows are Andersen double-hung Terratone with insulated glass, snap-in Colonial grilles, and screening. The many options include complete interior plastering.

SPECIAL FEATURES
American Barn is one of the very few companies that openly compare themselves to their competitors. The firm has printed up a comparison sheet that covers their array of standard items such as Perma-Shield windows, 2 x 6 cedar decking, all cedar exterior trim, and other features not included in standard packages of several competing firms.

RELATIVE SIZE/COST
The 1,168-square-foot Berkshire Barn model is about $26,000: $22 per foot for the complete closed-in building. The large Barn I Colonial with 2,352 square feet is about $47,000; $20 per square foot.

COMPANY INFORMATION
Separate color catalogs are available covering the more traditional American Barn homes and the more contemporary Habitat series.

PACIFIC FRONTIER HOMES, INC.

P.O. Box 1247
Fort Bragg, CA 95437
(707) 964-0204

PRODUCT RANGE

Pacific Frontier offers over thirty standard precut designs ranging from 300- and 400-square-foot one-room cabins to large two-story homes. The designs are contemporary and clean-lined. The Eagle's Nest, a plan featured in *Popular Science, Professional Builder,* and other magazines, has large glazing panels in the wall aligned with smaller panels at the roof eaves, multistory decks, and an interesting combination of angled and flat roof sections.

PREFAB COMPONENTS

Pacific precut packages include 4-inch construction redwood post and beam timbers, random-length t&g redwood siding and roof decking, exterior doors and glazed alu-minum sash required for a weathertight shell. Floor joists and subflooring (purchased locally to avoid shipping costs) are not included.

MATERIALS

Structural frames are exposed inside the house. The air-seasoned redwood posts are backed with 1½ x 6-inch random-length selected common redwood t&g planking, rough-sawn on one side. Insulation is 1½-inch double foil-faced urethane plus 15-pound saturated felt paper. Exterior siding laid over the insulation to make an on-site sandwich panel wall is 1 x 8-inch random-length clear kiln-dried vertical-grain redwood t&g planking. All interior partition walls are also solid redwood planking over redwood posts.

SPECIAL FEATURES

Typical of precut homes, Pacific's models can be erected without special skills or mechanical equipment. Posts and rafters are plumbed and braced over the owner's foundation and subfloor, covered with the first layer of redwood planking, then 4 x 8-foot panels of insulation, and tarpaper. After windows, roof windows, and doors are installed, finished roofing and exterior siding are applied. These straightforward construction methods have encouraged 60 percent of the company's clients to participate in the building process.

RELATIVE SIZE/COST

Pacific's Series III three-bedroom Cabrillo model with 1,658 square feet is approximately $42,000; $24 per square foot. The innovative Eagle's Nest model has 836 square feet on the first floor, 376 on the second, and costs approximately $28,000; $23 per square foot.

COMPANY INFORMATION

Pacific Frontier, now an independent company, started business as part of a research division of the Union Lumber Company in 1967, back when a book on prefab and precut homes would have been about twenty-five pages long. Thorough literature covering floor plans, a color brochure, detailed information on the performance of redwood, and costs is sent on request.

SHELTER-KIT, INC.
P.O. Box 1, 22 Mill Street
Tilton, NH 03276
(603) 934-4327

PRODUCT RANGE
Shelter-Kit sells several modular variations of two very basic buildings: a shed roof, 12 x 12-foot post and beam frame building and a steeply sloped design called the Lofthouse in 16 x 16- and 20 x 24-foot modules. "Shelter" is the key word. The company's best-known model, the basic, precut 12 x 12 Unit One, has been written up in virtually every how-to magazine.

PREFAB COMPONENTS
Working on a modular system, clients can order weatherized shell kits or frame-only kits in multiples ranging from utterly basic shelter to homes with four bedrooms, enclosed porches, and ample exterior deck space. All materials are precut and predrilled, and shipped in 100-pound packages for easy transport even to remote sites.

MATERIALS
The Unit One module consists of 4 x 4 Douglas fir posts, 2 x 10 spruce joists, 2 x 10 fir or southern yellow pine rafters, 2 x 4 stud fillers. Siding and flooring is 1 x 8 t&g pine with a ¾-inch AC plywood deck.

SPECIAL FEATURES
Main frame members are bolted together through predrilled holes, which makes the module self-squaring. While owner-builders with some building experience could easily duplicate this basic frame-with-sheathing plan, the simplicity of Shelter-Kit does make it relatively easy for even completely inexperienced owner-builders to work on their own home.

RELATIVE SIZE/COST
The basic 144-square-foot Unit One module is $1,300 for the frame kit, $3,900 for complete shell kit. The 16 x 16-foot Lofthouse models are roughly $3,400 for frame kit, and $7,700 for complete shell kit.

COMPANY INFORMATION
A brief flier is sent on request. Call or write for costs of complete plan options presented in detail.

SOLAR NORTHERN POST & BEAM, INC.

Box 64
Mansfield, PA 16933
(717) 549-6232

PRODUCT RANGE
Solar Northern offers nine standard precut post and beam homes ranging from a small contemporary design of 768 square feet to a large Colonial of 1,650 square feet. All frames, including custom designs, are based on traditional American architecture—for example, a two-story Cape with ell extension, and an elegant saltbox design.

PREFAB COMPONENTS
Solar Northern packages include the precut post and beam frame; insulating wall and roof panels; blueprints from the foundation up for building permits, and for soliciting estimates from contractors if you don't care to put the pieces together yourself; two days of on-site frame-raising supervision; and a complete list of materials needed to complete the house.

MATERIALS
Framing is either planed or rough-sawn white pine or hemlock joined with traditional, hand-cut mortise and tenon and lap joints. Foam-core insulating panels are composed of ½-inch wallboard to the inside, 3½ inches of urethane foam, and $^{7}/_{16}$-inch sheathing to the outside. The panels are installed on the frame exterior, exposing the massive timbers inside the house.

SPECIAL FEATURES
Following up on the idea of "Northern" structures, the firm offers two types of foam-core panels. Standard insulation of 3½ inches of foam can be replaced by 5½ inches of expanded polystyrene for R-30 ratings in cold climates.

RELATIVE SIZE/COST
Solar Northern frame packages range from roughly $6 to $9 per square foot. Frame with insulating panels range from roughly $12 to $18 per square foot. Complete closed-in shells range from $17 to $32 per square foot. The final

costs of finished homes vary widely depending on the degree of participation by the owners, and the choices of finishing materials. Solar Northern estimates final finished costs at between $29 and $54 per square foot.

COMPANY INFORMATION
The company has completed homes throughout the East and the Midwest. Estimates will be given for frame raising and panel application by the company. Most of their homes are designed for passive solar heating efficiency. On average, roughly half the heat requirements of Solar Northern homes is provided by the solar design built into the home. The company offers a brief but thorough and informative presentation, including current costs and information on design services, on request.

TIMBERPEG
Box 1500
Claremont, NH 03743
(603) 542-7762

PRODUCT RANGE
Timberpeg offers forty plans, many options, and design help in customizing and modifying standard plans. These frame structures have massive 8 x 12, 6 x 8, and 6 x 6 main members, with 6 x 6 and 4 x 6 collar ties and angled braces. Because conventional nails would be about as effective as toothpicks on timbers of this scale, Timberpeg uses mortise and tenon connections and tongue and fork joints held together with square oak pegs called trunnels. Timberpeg plans include Capes, saltboxes, and other traditional timber frame designs, as well as several more contemporary models, from the small Cluster Shed series, at 200 to 500 square feet, to sprawling, two-story homes of 3,500 square feet.

PREFAB COMPONENTS
Standard Timberpeg packages include frames, wall systems of pine panels or vinyl-faced Homasote board, and insulation. The New Hampshire plant ships 1 x 12 resawn pine siding with 1 x 3 battens. The North Carolina and Colorado plants ship exterior siding of ⅞-inch western red cedar. For an authentic Colonial facade Timberpeg also offers 4-inch to-the-weather clapboards with cedar trim. Kits also include complete roofs and all windows and doors, with special materials such as 3-inch Thermax insulating board on their Solar series homes.

MATERIALS
In addition to pine timbers, the kits include Andersen Perma-Shield windows with double glazing, screens, and snap-in grilles, prehung, pine frame, triple-hinged, six-panel and nine-light crossbuck exterior doors, Peachtree wood-framed, double-glazed, and tempered patio doors with fiber glass screens, and Roto roof windows.

SPECIAL FEATURES
Using an all-exterior wall system means that the massive timber frame is exposed inside the house. Wide frames at openings and the high R-value of rigid insulating boards make this possible. It's purely a matter of personal taste whether the massive but elegant timbers look better against a white background (even if it is vinyl instead of plaster) or pine planking.

RELATIVE SIZE/COST
Timberpeg's 2,624-square-foot Saltbox is roughly $74,000, or $28 per square foot. The company estimates a finished cost for the entire house of $150,000. A more contemporary frame from the Template series with 1,520 square feet is roughly $46,000, or $30 per square foot.

COMPANY INFORMATION
The company offers an array of plan books for $10, including all floor plans and endless interior and exterior photos, plus details on their solar homes, materials, and more. It's a bit high just to take a look. Try asking for a sample brochure to get started.

TIMBER SYSTEMS, INC.
P.O. Box 1496
Boulder, CO 80306
(303) 455-1100

PRODUCT RANGE
Timber Systems is run by Stewart Elliot, a timber frame designer and builder, and author of several books on the subject. The firm offers twenty-five different stock plans, and builds residential units from 600-square-foot cabins to 3,500-square-foot attached units and 6,000-square-foot custom homes.

PREFAB COMPONENTS
Although custom packages are available, typical Timber Systems kits include all timbers, laminated insulating sheathing panels applied outside the frame, air exchangers (because the finished house is so airtight it needs them to provide sufficient fresh air without heat loss), and all fasteners and sealers.

MATERIALS
Structural timbers are #1 air-dried Douglas fir in sizes from 3 x 6 angled braces to massive 8 x 20-inch girths. The frames are enclosed with Timber Systems' factory-assembled panels, laminations with interior Sheetrock (or wood options), a polyisocyanurate insulating core, and plywood exterior. Panels range from stock 4 x 8-foot 2½ inches thick for R-12 to 4 x 16-foot panels 8½ inches thick for a super-cold-climate R-65.

SPECIAL FEATURES
The need for air exchangers tells you that these homes are tight and incur little heat loss. In the Colorado area, typical annual heating and cooling costs are estimated at only 7 cents per square foot. That's an incredibly low $210 for a large, 3,000-square-foot house.

RELATIVE SIZE/COST
Average Timber Systems packages sell for $14 per square foot. When owner-builders are involved completed projects run between $22 and $30 per square foot for finished homes. Working regionally, the firm will assemble all timber frame bents (wall and roof timbers joined together) on your prepared foundation and first floor, and apply the sandwich panels for $4 per foot. A mobile crane is required for efficiency no matter who does the work, although an experienced rigger might get by with come-alongs, gin poles, and block and tackle. With mechanical help the firm calculates that 275 man-hours and 20 crane-hours are needed to assemble the site-delivered package for a 1,600-square-foot home, including frames, panels on walls, floor, and roof, plus all windows and doors.

COMPANY INFORMATION
Illustrated brochures of Timber Systems buildings with details on energy-efficient walls, materials, and assembly are sent on request. The firm ships nationally.

WICKES LUMBER
706 Deerpath Drive
Vernon Hills, IL 60061
(312) 367-3400

PRODUCT RANGE

Wickes offers twenty-two stock plans including L-shaped and in-line ranches, split-levels and leisure homes. Most are roughly 1,200 to 1,500 square feet. Within this framework Wickes provides an advanced, computer-assisted, custom-design process. Basic blueprints can accommodate major changes, for example, on interior partition layout, relocating doors and windows, adding insulation capacity, converting storage to living space.

PREFAB COMPONENTS

Wickes produces a basic shell package and an interior finishing package. The shell includes all wood framing, insulated sheathing, siding (plus paint and stain), all windows and doors, roof trusses with decking and finished roofing, rough flooring, insulation, and tubs and showers. The interior package includes drywall, paint, interior doors, and a kitchen cabinet package.

MATERIALS

Standard framing is kiln-dried 2 x 4 studding 16 inches on center with ½-inch plywood sheathing, and various wood sidings or aluminum clapboard. Walls include 3½ inches of fiber glass (with 6 inches in ceilings), and ½-inch drywall. The complete package includes such small but necessary details as gable end louvers, drip caps for openings, caulking, and nails.

SPECIAL FEATURES

The most unique feature about Wickes is its fully developed use of computers in design and construction. This allows detailed printouts of wall sections and floor plans, including an exact listing of materials.

RELATIVE SIZE/COST

Wickes home packages range from $10,000 to $25,000 for materials. Stressing the owner-builder option, the firm projects that 15 to 30 percent savings are possible even when working with a contractor. Adding land and mechanical costs for a completed home Wickes estimates that for $35,000 to $65,000 customers net a $50,000 to $125,000 home.

COMPANY INFORMATION

Wickes now offers computer-assisted design and construction planning that can translate layout changes into detailed alterations to material lists—even down to the number of nails required. The company provides guides on planning and financing, and serves clients nationally through Wickes Lumber Stores.

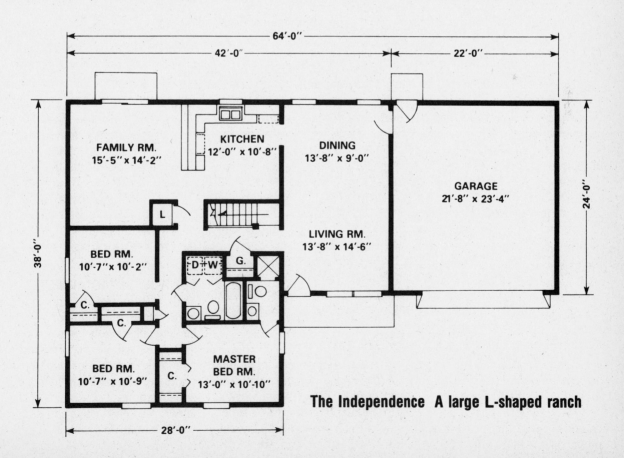

The Independence A large L-shaped ranch

YANKEE BARN HOMES

Star Route 3, Box 2
Grantham, NH 03753
(800) 258-9786
(603) 863-4545
(in New Hampshire)

PRODUCT RANGE

Yankee Barn offers timber frame homes, most with immense interior space suitable for free-flowing or partitioned interior layouts giving the feeling of a converted barn. Many stock plans are available, although virtually every home is individually planned. Gregory Lennox from the company writes, "Yankee Barn produces luxurious antique timber frame homes, ranging from 1,200 square feet to over 5,000 square feet, milled from authentic antique timbers reclaimed from historic structures."

PREFAB COMPONENTS

Standard home packages include reconditioned antique beams; panelized walls with exterior siding, vapor barrier, plywood sheathing, insulation, and paneled interior, complete with windows; exterior trim and doors; stressed-skin, insulated roof and floor panels and finished flooring (roof panels are felt-covered and ready for shingling); plus interior doors, stairs, balcony rails, and shutters.

MATERIALS

Yankee Barn can provide Douglas fir timbers, or cleaned but unstained antique timbers. Panelized walls exposing the frame inside have vertical, rough-sawn, kiln-dried, shiplap eastern white pine, prefinished with Olympic stain. The company offers several options with all finishing materials. The panel includes Tyvek Housewrap, ½-inch CDX sheathing, 2-inch or greater Thermax insulation, ⅝-inch Douglas fir interior paneling, and double-glazed windows with half screens. The 3¼-inch Thermax is standard on roof panels, prepaneled on the inside. Finished flooring is 1 x 6 random-length yellow pine.

SPECIAL FEATURES

Although these homes can be built by experienced owners, the company literature stresses working with a general contractor or supervising the job yourself, hiring subcontractors to do the work. Because of the component assembly, Yankee Barn estimates that a four-member crew with a supervisor can erect their most popular design, the 48-foot Prairie Barn, in ten days, including offloading.

RELATIVE SIZE/COST

The 48-foot Prairie Barn model with 3,226 square feet of usable living space has a projected cost of $170,000 to $195,000 above foundation; roughly $56 per square foot. The firm also makes a 984-square-foot Studio Barn and many other models, up to a 4,414-square-foot stock plan.

COMPANY INFORMATION

Yankee Barn provides an elaborate information portfolio for $12, including all models, specifications, and rendered views of exteriors, plus a short full-color booklet with photos of interiors and exteriors, a specifications booklet, and price sheet. Yankee Barn is a member of the National Association of Home Builders and the Manufactured Housing Council.

MANUFACTURED HOMES

ACORN STRUCTURES, INC.

Box 250
Concord, MA 01742
(617) 369-4111

PRODUCT RANGE

Acorn produces some fifty basic plans, generally of contemporary design, including a series of solar efficient houses such as the one shown above. The firm is a true national manufacturer with regional sales offices (most with full model homes) in Maryland, New York, Florida, Pennsylvania, Colorado, and California.

PREFAB COMPONENTS

Standard specifications include all framing, finished siding and soffits, windows and doors, finished roofing, exterior decks, interior partitions, stairs, trim, all hardware, and prefinished cabinets.

MATERIALS

Acorn uses double pressure-treated 2 x 6 sills, 2 x 10 joists 16 inches on center with ⅝-inch tongue and groove decking. Walls are 2 x 4 framing with ½-inch CDX sheathing. Standard siding is 1 x 4 #3 tongue and groove cedar with options for #1 cedar or shakes. Windows are Pella wood frame with screens and storm sash. An extremely detailed specifications list follows through with this type of high quality throughout the house.

SPECIAL FEATURES

Acorn offers a series of solar-efficient homes with a heat collection and warm air distribution system built in, and with active solar backup. Solar domestic hot water systems are also offered.

RELATIVE SIZE/COST

Small two-level homes, one roughly 1,000 square feet with two bedrooms and a bath, is $60,000 to $70,000 for the finished home, including foundation, all mechanical work and major appliances, less land. For between $110,000 and $120,000 finished costs, Acorn produces homes from 1,600 to 1,800 square feet with three or four bedrooms. Large models with solar options range well over $200,000 for roughly 3,500 to 4,000 square feet. The full plans portfolio is available for $10.

COMPANY INFORMATION

Acorn can provide design brochures and a detailed specification sheet that lays out every bit of material, and all the options, in their home designs. A separate brochure is available for Acorn's Solar series homes.

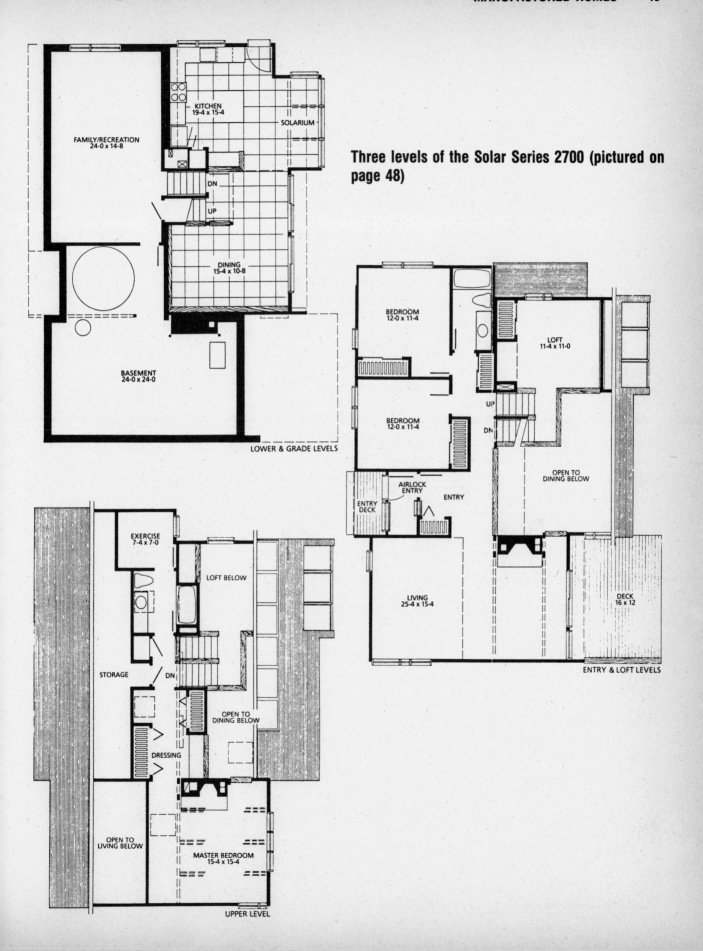

FAMILY/RECREATION
24-0 x 14-8

KITCHEN
19-4 x 15-4

SOLARIUM

DN

UP

DINING
15-4 x 10-8

BASEMENT
24-0 x 24-0

LOWER & GRADE LEVELS

Three levels of the Solar Series 2700 (pictured on page 48)

BEDROOM
12-0 x 11-4

LOFT
11-4 x 11-0

BEDROOM
12-0 x 11-4

UP

DN

OPEN TO
DINING BELOW

AIRLOCK
ENTRY

ENTRY
DECK

ENTRY

LIVING
25-4 x 15-4

DECK
16 x 12

ENTRY & LOFT LEVELS

EXERCISE
7-4 x 7-0

LOFT BELOW

STORAGE

DN

OPEN TO
DINING BELOW

DRESSING

OPEN TO
LIVING BELOW

MASTER BEDROOM
15-4 x 15-4

UPPER LEVEL

CARDINAL INDUSTRIES, INC.

10 Plumosa Drive
Cassleberry, FL 32707
(305) 831-5676

PRODUCT RANGE

Cardinal builds a series of low-cost prefabs in modules. Basic, three-module homes—one for living and dining, one for bed and kitchen, and one for second bed and bath—may be added on to. Extra modules for full master bed and second bath, a family room, etc., are available. Modules are 14-foot widths.

PREFAB COMPONENTS

Standard features include rough-sawn cedar exterior siding and trim, aluminum soffits, fiber glass roof shingles, double-insulated windows, insulated metal-clad doors, all caulking and insulation (R-11 in walls and floor with R-26 in ceilings), smoke detectors, ground fault breakers in baths, deadbolt locks, fire-rated wallboard interiors, carpeting.

MATERIALS

Cardinal uses conventional framing to completely prebuild modules delivered to the site and hoisted by crane into place on the foundation. All homes have General Electric heating and air-conditioning equipment and kitchen appliances. Baths have a one-piece tub/shower combination.

SPECIAL FEATURES

Cardinal supplies a 200-page maintenance and repair manual for every home and a "Master Parts Kit," an overall repair package with extra caulk, paint, etc.

RELATIVE SIZE/COST

Less land, Cardinal's basic Series 2000 with one bedroom and bath is roughly $24,000, including plans, site visit, 28-inch concrete block foundation, backfilling, soil treatment, front stoop, plumbing connections, 30 feet of water laterals, and 10 feet of sewer laterals. Series 4000 models with two bedrooms and two baths are roughly $41,000. Master bed modules are about $10,000.

COMPANY INFORMATION

Cardinal sells nationally and offers information on financing, their Builder's Warranty, Homeowner's Guide, and Homeowner's Master Parts Kits on request.

DELUXE HOMES OF PENNSYLVANIA, INC.
P.O. Box 323
Berwick, PA 18603
(717) 752-5914

Colonial

Rustic

Traditional

Tudor

PRODUCT RANGE
DeLuxe Homes sells completely manufactured homes with finished walls and roof, plus all mechanical systems and finished interiors. An extensive line of prefab homes includes single-family homes from 900 to 2,000 square feet designed as ranches, split-levels, Capes, split-foyers, and traditional two-story homes; also town house models with either wood or steel frame from 900 to 5,000 square feet.

PREFAB COMPONENTS
A typical package includes complete framing and sheathing, R-13 wall insulation and siding, interior wallboard painted and trimmed, finished roofing, complete pvc plumbing, a 200-amp electrical service with copper wiring, light fixtures, and smoke detectors, kitchen cabinets and fixtures, and complete baths, with all windows and doors.

MATERIALS
DeLuxe provides a detailed specifications sheet (HUD-FHA Document 2005) that lists exactly what is offered. Basic components are: standard 2 x 4 framing on walls with ½-inch sheathing, .019-gauge aluminum siding, double-glazed, double-hung windows, steel-clad, insulated-core exterior doors, ½-inch drywall prefinished interior, ¾-inch floor decking with ¼-inch overlay over 2 x 10 joists, with R-19 insulation, cushioned vinyl floors in kitchen and baths, with carpet on ⅜-inch padding elsewhere. Baths are equipped with one-piece fiber glass molded fixtures. The spec sheet covers details of chimney flues, cabinet finish, and even performance characteristics of heating systems.

SPECIAL FEATURES
DeLuxe offers many options, including energy-efficient fireplaces, sun deck extensions, 2-foot extension modules to standard floor plans, R-30 roof insulation, individual room thermostats for control of electric baseboard heat, and entire packages of energy-efficient features.

RELATIVE SIZE/COST
Quotes for specific models and options are given on request. DeLuxe homes range from $22 to $30 per square foot.

COMPANY INFORMATION
DeLuxe sells in the eastern United States from West Virginia to Maine. The firm works through builders and developers, and offers full installation services from two manufacturing plants. Information is sent on request. DeLuxe's spec sheet is an interesting look at the full range of materials in a completely prefab home.

FLEETWOOD ENTERPRISES, INC.

3125 Myers Street
P.O. Box 7638
Riverside, CA 92523
(714) 351-3500

PRODUCT RANGE

Fleetwood builds complete homes in its plant, then brings them to your site. That used to be called mobile housing. Now it's called manufactured, or, if you like a real euphemism, site-delivered. Fleetwood is a leading manufacturer, producing roughly thirty thousand homes a year in a wide variety of sizes, with top-of-the-line models offering over 1,600 square feet.

PREFAB COMPONENTS

Aside from the low cost, manufactured homes offer completely prefinished houses. A typical Fleetwood home has a shingled roof, a slate-tile entry, a cathedral-ceiling living room, paneling, carpeting, and drapes, a chandelier in the dining room, all built-in appliances, a wood-burning fireplace, and more.

MATERIALS

Fleetwood homes are fully shop-built, following increasingly stringent government standards for the industry. Structural design includes a 40 psf floor live load, minimum bedroom size of 70 square feet, 22-inch closet depth, two exit doors for fire safety, and other standards customary in many stick-built development houses.

SPECIAL FEATURES

Fleetwood is an accessible company with twenty-five manufactur-

ing plants across the U.S. and Canada. About half their homeowners live in park communities (formerly called trailer parks), while the other half live on private sites. The firm has participated in some interesting housing experiments. *Professional Builder* magazine covered a development in Yorba Linda, California, that mixed mobile and stick-built homes.

RELATIVE SIZE/COST

Fleetwood homes range from $8,000 to over $30,000 for top-of-

the-line models. *Professional Builder* reports that Fleetwood-manufactured homes (roughly $100,000 with land for roughly 1,500 square feet) were priced at least $25,000 less than similar stick-built homes in the same area. With innovative use of an AWWF (all-weather wood foundation) full-height foundation, it is possible to combine owner-builder–prepared foundations and site-delivered homes to achieve very low cost homes with a lot of usable space.

COMPANY INFORMATION

Fleetwood offers a complete plan package and extensive information on their construction methods and the manufactured-housing industry on request. Fleetwood has been a Fortune 500 company for the last five years.

GALAXY HOMES, INC.

502 5th Street NW
P.O. Box 219
Dyersville, IA 52040
(319) 875-2421

PRODUCT RANGE

Galaxy offers fifty different floor plans for completely factory built homes with stock widths of 23 feet 6 inches and 27 feet 6 inches, including duplex and fourplex units. Standard lengths range from 34 to 60 feet. Styles are conventional and simplified: a long rectangle with low-slope roof that may become known as the "manufactured style." But the firm offers modifications on the most basic plan, including ranches, raised ranches, and tri-levels.

PREFAB COMPONENTS

Galaxy provides finished homes with closed-in, insulated, wood-frame shell, textured hardboard lap siding, and textured wallboard inside; carpeting for living room, bedrooms, and halls, complete kitchen cabinets, gas range, refrigerator, stove vent hood, complete baths; plus heating, plumbing, and electrical systems—a true turnkey home.

MATERIALS

Galaxy uses 2 x 10 floor joists 16 inches on center with 1 x 3 bridging and ½-inch subflooring plus ⅝-inch particleboard underlayment with Armstrong vinyl flooring. Walls are 7 feet 6 inches high with standard 2 x 4 wall construction (R-11 with an option for R-19), including ½-inch wallboard inside, and 12-inch prefinished Boise lap siding outside over sheathing. Roofing is framed with 2 x 4 truss rafters (R-30 with an option for R-41), ½-inch decking, double-cover felt paper, and 235-pound asphalt shingles. Generally, all construction materials are comparable to those found on conventional, site-built, "custom" stick-frame homes that many consider superior to factory homes.

SPECIAL FEATURES

Galaxy prefinished homes (including two coats of sand-textured paint inside) can be ready for occupancy in only two to three days (including full mechanical systems) after delivery to the owner-prepared site.

RELATIVE SIZE/COST

The firm's manufactured homes cost between $40,000 and $90,000. Specific prices are quoted on request. The company services fifteen states from three manufacturing plants in Dyersville, Iowa; Greeley, Colorado; and Victor, New York.

COMPANY INFORMATION

Information will be sent on request. Galaxy is a member of the National Association of Home Builders.

MARLEY CONTINENTAL HOMES

1900 Johnson Drive
Mission Woods, KS 66205
(913) 362-5440

PRODUCT RANGE

Marley's very conventional-looking two-story Colonial (pictured) might help change some minds about manufactured housing. It was built in large modular pieces in the plant and trucked to the site for assembly. Marley makes endless models in styles ranging from classic Colonial to western ranch, from 900 to 3,000 square feet, and multifamily housing. In late 1984 they unveiled a unique line of Victorian-styled manufactured homes, the first on the market. These very interesting homes mark a significant step for factory-built housing, combining low-cost, efficient building technology with classic, distinctive American designs—definitely not the homogenous development house.

PREFAB COMPONENTS

Factory-built modular units are 90 to 95 percent complete when they leave the plant. A small ranch house would arrive at the site in only two units, while a large Colonial two-story is built in four to six units. Although stock plans offer great variety, buyers select not only home style and design, but carpet grade and color, wallpapers, kitchen cabinets, countertops, and additional optional items such as fireplaces and intercom-security systems.

MATERIALS

Marley's New England region plant turns out all homes with triple-glazed windows. Double glazing is standard elsewhere. Marley builds conventional stick frames but offers just about any kind of finish or material you could want, inside and out: wood, vinyl siding, finish brick, stucco.

SPECIAL FEATURES

Marley builds homes at locations in Nashua, New Hampshire; Roanoke, Virginia; and Haines City, Florida, and has just opened a plant in Kansas City, Kansas. Regional production helps the company to deliver complete homes in good or bad weather generally within thirty days of final orders and clearances. There thus will be no material or labor price increases, which are common on stick-built, on-site construction jobs.

RELATIVE SIZE/COST

Costs vary widely depending on materials, cost of utility connections, and other factors, but Marley estimates a spread of complete homes from the low $50s to $300,000.

COMPANY INFORMATION

Marley's brief color brochure with a sample home floor plan and pictorial view is sent on request. They also offer free tours of their manufacturing plants during working hours, so you can see the huge jig machines and modular production methods in operation.

NATIONWIDE HOMES, INC.

P.O. Box 5511
Martinsville, VA 24115
(703) 632-7101

PRODUCT RANGE

Nationwide offers a wide range of fully shop built homes in two basic categories: a Standard series, including economical starter homes from 860 square feet in ranch, split-level, Cape, two-story Colonial, and tri-level styles; and the Williamsburg Heritage series—larger homes with more steeply sloped roofs, and more options available.

PREFAB COMPONENTS

Nationwide's homes are technically conventional code-complying modular houses. So even though the house is completely fabricated in the plant, the materials used are the same as if the home had been site-built. Nationwide builds homes in halves, completely framed and sheathed, with full mechanical systems, cabinets, wall covering—the works. Factory crews fasten the halves together on the owner-prepared foundation, and install final siding and roofing.

MATERIALS

Floors are 2 x 8 and 2 x 10 joists, with 2 x 4 walls and 3/8-inch plywood sheathing, Sheetrock walls, solid wood trim, fiber glass insulation.

SPECIAL FEATURES

In the Williamsburg series, designs include full cathedral ceilings, choices of light fixtures, and hardboard, vinyl, aluminum, Texture 1-11, or cedar siding.

RELATIVE SIZE/COST

Prices are quoted for specific models after consultation with customers. Prices for complete houses start at $29,000.

COMPANY INFORMATION

Nationwide's information packet includes a color brochure that shows step by step exactly how these houses are fabricated, shipped, assembled, and finished. It is a fascinating process, combining mass production and hand work. Nationwide sells through dealers in nine eastern states. Shipping is by company-owned trucks. The firm is a member of the National Association of Home Builders and the Council of Home Manufacturers.

NORTH AMERICAN HOUSING CORP.

P.O. Box 145
Point of Rocks, MD 21777
(301) 948-8500

PRODUCT RANGE

North American manufactures over fifty standard models of completed prefab homes in a wide variety of sizes and styles, including split-levels, town houses, contemporaries, and vacation homes.

PREFAB COMPONENTS

Typical North American homes include a completely framed shell with finished floors, walls, and roofing, all partitions, kitchen cabinets, bath fixtures, full mechanical systems, and even light fixtures.

MATERIALS

The homes are built in 24-inch modules with 2 x 8 joists 16 inches on center, and ⅝-inch underlayment of t&g decking. Finished floors are padded carpet and resilient sheet flooring in kitchens, baths, and foyers. Standard 2 x 4 studwalls carry an R-13 rating with an option for R-19, with texture-finish aluminum siding or Texture 1-11 plywood. Windows are Andersen Perma-Shield Narroline double-hungs with double glazing, screens, and grilles. Triple glazing is optional. Exterior doors are 1¾-inch recessed panel with sidelights. Interiors are finished with painted ½-inch drywall. Kitchens are equipped with Kitchen Kompact cabinets.

SPECIAL FEATURES

The company has set up complete model homes at their manufacturing plants in Maryland and Virginia. An extensive list of options is available, including energy-saving packages of R-30 ceilings and triple-glazed windows. Kitchen planning guides enable you to select cabinet components.

RELATIVE SIZE/COST

North American homes range from about $17,000 complete for small homes to $35,000 and $40,000 for larger models. Energy-saving packages add roughly $700 to $1,000 to each design.

COMPANY INFORMATION

The firm currently serves Maryland, Delaware, New Jersey, Virginia, West Virginia, and Pennsylvania. Sample floor plans and elevation views will be sent on request, with an extensive list of options, alternative materials, and costs. North American is a member of the National Association of Home Builders.

NORTHERN HOMES
51 Glenwood Avenue
Glens Falls, NY 12801
(518) 798-6007

PRODUCT RANGE
Northern manufactures many types of wood frame homes, including domes, log homes, and pole buildings, in many styles, including clean-lined contemporaries, ranch houses, and an extensive line of elegant Colonial homes. Their homes range from roughly 1,000 to 6,000 square feet of living space.

PREFAB COMPONENTS
Although over 95 percent of Northern's many stock designs are customized to some degree, all models are panelized—shop-built in large sections, then shipped to the site and erected. The only items not included in a standard Northern home package are foundation work, mechanical systems, and interior finishing (wallboard, painting, etc.). Everything else, from windows and shutters to stairs, exterior deck, and all hardware, is included.

MATERIALS
Joists, sills, and girders are all kiln-dried for stability. Framing is sheathed with $7/16$-inch Aspenite, with $1/2$-inch CDX plywood on the roof. Siding is 4-inch to the weather pine clapboard, or vinyl, aluminum, or cedar. Windows are Andersen Perma-Shield with insulated glass and screens. Exterior doors are Peachtree steel-clad insulated (for R-14), $1\frac{3}{4}$ inches thick, prehung on pine jambs. Exterior decking is $5/4$ pressure-treated t&g.

SPECIAL FEATURES
Contrary to the canard that when homes are manufactured you can pick only plan A or plan B with no changes or extras, Northern can provide a great degree of customization and still deliver the benefits of shop assembly—even a swinging dog entrance door built into an overhead garage door.

RELATIVE SIZE/COST

It won't help you much to know that the price range for Northern homes is $75,000 to $750,000. Specific quotes are made on request.

COMPANY INFORMATION

Northern Homes sells through a dealer network mainly in the East, running from Virginia through New England, although they have shipped homes to North Carolina and Ohio. The firm's general specification sheet covers every part of the many different homes. Plans are presented on sheets with several pictures of the house on one side and a clear, detailed floor plan on the other. The company's president, Michael Carusone, is a past president of the Home Manufacturers Council, and the firm is a member of the National Association of Home Manufacturers and the National Chamber of Commerce. They have been in the building business since 1946.

PACIFIC BUILDINGS, INC.

P.O. Drawer C
Marks, MS 38646
(601) 326-8104

PRODUCT RANGE

Pacific Buildings' specialty is panelizing and manufacturing major sections in the shop for almost any set of plans. Frank Wright from Pacific Buildings writes, "We custom manufacture to anyone's plans, and are unlimited in size, style, and square footage of plans using wood construction." This ability should dispel another misconception about manufactured housing—that special jigs, templates, and sophisticated framing machines in the factory can produce only one size and one style of home. New home-manufacturing machinery is fast at paneling 8-foot wall sections but can easily produce other sizes with a variety of interior and exterior finishes.

PREFAB COMPONENTS

Typical Pacific Buildings kits include completely panelized walls with framing, sheathing, and siding ready for interior finishing; roof and floor trusses made of gang-nailed dimensional timbers, cabinets for kitchens and baths, and all exterior trim.

MATERIALS

Standard dimensional timber can be combined with a wide variety of finishing materials.

SPECIAL FEATURES

Pacific Buildings does not supply any standard plans.

RELATIVE SIZE/COST

On average, Pacific Buildings' manufactured packages range from $8 to $12 per square foot, which the company estimates represents roughly one third of the overall costs for a completely finished house.

COMPANY INFORMATION

Pacific will send details on request. The firm is a member of the National Association of Home Builders. Company president S. A. Walter recently served as chairman of that organization's Home Manufacturers Council.

REDMAN HOMES, INC.

2550 Walnut Hill
Dallas, TX 75229
(214) 353-3600

PRODUCT RANGE

Redman is one of the largest and oldest home-manufacturing firms in the country. They have an extensive product line, sold under too many different brand names to be listed here. Redman is the only major producer of manufactured housing *and* general building products. Since 1937, when the first Redman mobile home was built, and through World War II, when Redman built prefab emergency military housing, and cabinets for B-17 bombers, the firm has turned out nearly 400,000 homes. Their completely shop built homes come in conventional trailer widths, double widths joined together, and more. Before you think this company sells inexpensive housing with no style, note that *Family Circle* magazine named one Redman unit "Home of the Year," for packing a lot of style and convenience into 1,000 square feet and pricing the home at an affordable $25,000. The homes range from 600 to 2,400 square feet.

PREFAB COMPONENTS

Redman homes are entirely factory-built and delivered in prefinished sections, with siding, roofing, cabinets, floor covering, mechanical systems, and even smoke detectors.

MATERIALS

Although many choices are available, the Redman award-winning home includes Armstrong sheet flooring, Intertherm heating and cooling systems, all-copper wiring (not low-cost and potentially hazardous aluminum), Whirlpool and Magic Chef kitchen appliances, a greenhouse window, and fiber glass wall insulation that exceeds HUD standards.

SPECIAL FEATURES

Redman says their homes can be built for as much as 50 percent less than site-built homes of comparable size and quality, a savings due to the efficiency of mass production.

RELATIVE SIZE/COST

Redman will quote prices on request; their emphasis is on low-cost homes, with extremely low costs per square foot.

COMPANY INFORMATION

One of the reasons Redman can deliver factory-built homes at low prices is regional production. The firm has eighteen manufacturing plants around the country, and can prebuild your home in your area, which also cuts shipping. They sell through some 1,400 retail locations. The firm has catalogs of their many series of homes, and good information on the prefab system, including quality details such as ground fault circuit interrupters (extra-safe, quick-tripping circuit breakers) in all bath and kitchen outlets.

PANELIZED HOMES

AFFORDABLE LUXURY HOMES, INC.

Highway 224 West
P.O. Box 288
Markle, IN 46770
(219) 758-2141

PRODUCT RANGE

Affordable Luxury Homes (a contradiction in terms put forward to get their point across) builds an extensive line of prefab houses, but differs from many manufacturers in that they specialize in a building system, which can be applied to stock plans, and to elaborate, custom-designed homes as illustrated. The homes are sold in two basic packages: open panel with frame and sheathing, and closed panel, which includes a completely finished panel with sheathing outside and wallboard inside sandwiching a solid core of expanded polystyrene insulation.

PREFAB COMPONENTS

Open panel packages include pre-cut framing with rough openings and sheathing, partition walls, floor joists and decking, roof trusses and finished roofing, insulated windows, doors, plus stairs, sill sealer, and other details required for a closed-in shell. The closed-panel package adds finished interior wallboard over prewired walls.

MATERIALS

Affordable uses standard 2 x 4 framing as required by code. However, I got a sample of the styrene core panel, with wallboard on one side and sheathing on the other, stood on it, piled concrete blocks on it, and nothing happened, which is exactly what you want a wall to do when it is loaded with rafters and shingles and a foot of snow. Exterior sheathing is $7/16$-inch waferboard; decking is $5/8$- or $3/4$-inch tongue and groove ply. Windows are double-glazed aluminum frame; doors are insulated and steel-clad.

SPECIAL FEATURES

Affordable's unique wall panel is relatively lightweight and easy to assemble. Company crews can completely close in a house in only a day or two, at which point it is already wired, and ready for taping and painting.

RELATIVE SIZE/COST

A typical plan with roughly 1,600 square feet is approximately $11,000 for the basic open panel package, $19,000 for that package set up, $13,000 for the insulated closed-panel package, $23,000 for that package erected. The firm estimates total costs for the completed home to be between $45,000 and $56,000.

COMPANY INFORMATION

Affordable Homes ships thirty stock plans nationally and has built customized designs from New Jersey to California. The firm is a member of the Home Manufacturer's Council of the NAHB. Several case histories show an expected 60 percent savings on energy costs with the unique foam-core building system.

A front elevation of a customized home built by Affordable Luxury Homes

AMERICAN STANDARD HOMES CORP.

700 Commerce Court
P.O. Box 4908
Martinsville, VA 24115
(703) 638-3991

PRODUCT RANGE

American Standard is a large firm making panelized homes. They have produced over 15,000 to date, in some 350 different models. In addition to multifamily buildings and commercial buildings, the company produces five series of homes: vacation homes from 800 to 2,000 square feet, custom-designed homes from 2,850 to 3,500 square feet, stock plans in over two hundred different styles from 1,200 to 2,800 square feet, and two lines of basic starter homes from about 800 to 1,300 square feet.

PREFAB COMPONENTS

American Standard packages include all panelized framing to complete a closed-in shell. Options include cabinets, windows, appliances, complete mechanical systems, and more. A typical job runs about five days, starting with decking, then panelized walls with Celotex sheathing and interior partitions, with a shingled roof in place at the end of the second day.

MATERIALS

American Standard Homes are built with precut floor systems, roof trusses, prehung doors, and conventional studwall construction, all panelized in the firm's 130,000-square-foot plant.

SPECIAL FEATURES

This firm's extensive line of standard plans offers the economy of panelized construction in the widest possible variety of floor plans and elevations.

RELATIVE SIZE/COST

American Standard's models range from roughly $12,000 to $50,000. Specific costs are quoted on request.

COMPANY INFORMATION

This firm is a public corporation, founded in 1968. American Standard ships east of the Mississippi, and has recently begun to ship overseas. The company sells through a network of forty-five field offices. The main office should be able to provide the name of a reasonably local builder. American Standard is a member of the National Association of Home Builders and the National Manufactured Housing Association.

CHASE BARLOW LUMBER CO.

P.O. Box 32038
4600 Robards Lane
Louisville, KY 40232
(502) 452-2686

PRODUCT RANGE

Chase Barlow manufactures custom and standard plan homes for sale regionally, including single-family and multifamily homes. Seven standard plans are marketed under the name Summitbilt, ranging from small starter homes to standard-size, two-story units, all factory-built with panels ranging up to 40 feet.

PREFAB COMPONENTS

Chase Barlow packages exterior and interior walls, decks, roofing, windows and doors, trim, and options for insulation, triple-glazed openings, complete kitchens and baths, and many material options, such as birch-veneer doors.

MATERIALS

Standard construction specs include 2 x 4 studwall 16 inches on center with ½-inch sheathing over let-in corner bracing, with framed openings and windows and doors installed—a full panelized wall. Aluminum frame windows include a thermal break, screens, insulated glass, in white or bronze finish. Exterior doors are prehung metal-clad and foam-filled, with locksets keyed alike for front and back doors.

SPECIAL FEATURES

Chase Barlow introduced steel-toothed-plate connectors for wood truss construction in Kentucky, and uses the system to produce floor frame trusses that can clear span up to 32 feet. Panelized housing components can be engineered at the plant to be erected by light mobile crane, or manually.

RELATIVE SIZE/COST

Prices are quoted on request. Chase's standard models start at $5,000.

COMPANY INFORMATION

Chase can supply complete specifications and a brochure detailing the panelizing process on request.

DELTA INDUSTRIES, INC.

1951 Galaxie Drive
Columbus, OH 43207
(614) 445-9634

PRODUCT RANGE

Delta manufactures a wide range of homes, all built around a very interesting structural sandwich panel with an insulating foam core. The panelized homes are contemporary, with potential for partial earth-sheltering, and floor plans with roughly 1,000 to 3,000 square feet.

PREFAB COMPONENTS

Delta offers three basic purchasing plans, for homeowners, builders, and custom designs.

MATERIALS

Basic Delta construction consists of panels made with polystyrene foam 3½, 5½, or 7½ inches thick, sandwiched between layers of ⅜-inch waferboard. The panels can be used for walls 8 to 16 feet high. As roof panels they can clear span from 4 to 16 feet, depending on deflection limits and foam-core thickness.

SPECIAL FEATURES

Delta's foam-core system can be applied to almost any type of wood frame construction, including earth-sheltered building.

RELATIVE SIZE/COST

Prices for stock plan homes are quoted on request.

COMPANY INFORMATION

For details about the panelized system, write or call Delta. They have information brochures that are a bit technical, but do convey the design applications and performance of this unique material.

DELTEC HOMES
537 Hazel Mill Road
P.O. Box 6931
Asheville, NC 28806
(704) 253-0483

PRODUCT RANGE
Deltec makes panelized, nearly circular homes—polygons made of factory-built panels. Sizes range from 500 to over 2,000 square feet, with ten to twenty standard 8-foot exterior panels. For example, their 1,200-square-foot model has fifteen sides. Five models are commonly used as residences, although a small 500-square-foot unit can be used as a connector unit—a guest house, game room, or office. All units can be connected and stacked up to three stories.

PREFAB COMPONENTS
All exterior wall sections are prefabricated at the Deltec plant, including windows, doors, insulation, and siding. Floor sections are pie-shaped panels, also prebuilt. The package includes roof shingles, exterior decking, insulation, and all materials to close in the shell.

MATERIALS
Deltec uses standard 2 x 4 studwall construction with $5/8$-inch rough-sawn board and batten Douglas fir siding, $3\frac{1}{2}$ inches of fiber glass insulation, and treated sills for slab construction. Exterior doors are insulated steel-clad and aluminum-frame double-glazed sliders. Roof construction is kiln-dried 2 x 6 trusses with galvanized truss plates and framing anchors covered with $5/8$-inch CD exterior grade sheathing with $3/8$-inch soffits. Trusses radiate out from a center compression ring anchor, creating a hut-type roof with a center vent cap. Shop-built floor panels are built around 10-inch beams with $5/8$-inch CD deck and $3/8$-inch soffit enclosing R-11 fiber glass insulation. Exterior decking is pressure-treated pine.

SPECIAL FEATURES

Deltec Polyrama framing allows 360-degree glazing exposure and wraparound decking. The firm also offers architectural service for customizing designs, and several materials options, such as western red cedar exterior siding.

RELATIVE SIZE/COST

Complete packages excluding mechanical systems and interior finishing range from $10 to $15 per square foot. A twelve-side, 32-foot-diameter model with 752 square feet is roughly $11,000 over a slab, and $21,000 for a two-story model; roughly $14 per square foot. The 39-foot-diameter models with 1,181 square feet are roughly $15,000 over a slab, and $30,000 for two-story construction; roughly $13 per square foot.

COMPANY INFORMATION

Deltec provides straightforward literature describing their Polyrama homes on request. Even the small color flier shows several photos, and enough of the construction details to give a good idea of the design.

HAIDA HIDE, INC.
19237 Aurora Avenue N
Seattle, WA 98133
(206) 546-4183

PRODUCT RANGE
This firm takes its name from the Haida Indians, a tribe of the Pacific Northwest renowned for their long-beam building and carving, including some of the longest dugout canoes known. The company produces chalet homes with unique outward-sloping sidewalls. The design is about halfway between a conventional peak roof house and an A-frame. Haida Hide make seventeen standard models, which can be modified with one or two dormers (bedroom-size), ranging from 20 x 24-foot cabins to nearly 1,500-square-foot homes with three bedrooms.

PREFAB COMPONENTS
Standard package materials include precut joists and subfloor, panelized exterior and interior walls with kiln-dried framing, CDX plywood sheathing, and beveled cedar siding, prefab roof trusses with sheathing, insulation, pre-hung doors and slider windows, all hardware, and interior wallboard and trim. Cedar decking, mechanical systems, and other options are available on quote.

MATERIALS
Haida Hide precuts select cedar exterior paneling, offered also on inside walls, insulated glass, R-11 wall construction with R-30 ceilings, all kiln-dried framing with 2 x 8 joists and ¾-inch t&g underlayment. Exterior panelized walls are sheathed with ⅜-inch CDX plywood. Deluxe packages include 2 x 6 t&g select hemlock roof decking, insulated skylights for kitchen and bath, rough-sawn cedar pan-

eling in all rooms except baths and closets.

SPECIAL FEATURES
All load-bearing frames are cut from old-growth, select Douglas fir, kiln-dried for stability. The firm estimates that two people can assemble the precut house following detailed blueprints.

RELATIVE SIZE/COST
Chalet models, 20 feet wide with roughly 780 square feet, cost about $19,000 with single dormer;

$24 per square foot. Large models in 24-foot widths with 2,000 square feet are $45,000; $22 per square foot.

COMPANY INFORMATION
Basic information covering Haida Hide designs and construction is sent on request. The firm has shipped internationally, and generally can deliver within four weeks of receipt of order. Model homes with the patented chalet construction are open for viewing at the Seattle offices.

NORTHERN COUNTIES LUMBER, INC.

P.O. Box 97
Upperville, VA 22176
(703) 592-3232

PRODUCT RANGE

Northern Counties offers eighteen stock plans in three styles: recreational, which are small, vacation-type homes; traditional, which are generally Colonial; and contemporary, which are clean-lined designs with large amounts of glazing. Small cabins are 20 x 28, while some of the larger homes are close to 3,000 square feet.

PREFAB COMPONENTS

Northern includes all materials needed to build a closed-in shell, including windows and doors, and interior wall partitions.

MATERIALS

All framing is kiln-dried, covered with rigid insulating board. Their most interesting model, the Clifton, is a panelized earth-sheltered home built on an AWWF system. Treated 2 x 10 studwalls are panelized with ¾-inch treated plywood, glued and nailed, then covered with 6-mil polyethylene and 9 inches of gravel backfill. Floors are treated 2 x 6 grade beams on gravel footings with ⅝-inch t&g AWWF subflooring glued and nailed, set so the crawl space can be used as a heat-distributing plenum. Laminated beams are used on earth-sheltered roofs with sprayed and trowled Bentonite system waterproofing, plastic sheeting, and a 12- to 18-inch earth cover. For those unfamiliar with earth sheltering, moderate temperatures below ground offer astonishing energy savings, protection from storms, isolation from noise, and the opportunity to preserve a special building site.

SPECIAL FEATURES

Northern is one of the few companies to apply modern panelizing technology to earth-sheltered design. These homes are usually custom built or owner designed and built. Relatively flat sites can

be regraded with earth berms for earth sheltering, although sloped sites are more compatible.

RELATIVE SIZE/COST
Full shells for smaller models such as the Woodland with 560 square feet cost roughly $8,000 for prefab materials and $11,500 for the erected shell; $14 and $20 per square foot respectively. The large Braddock traditional design, roughly 56 x 28 with 1,568 square feet, is $21,000 for shell materials and $28,000 for materials plus installation; $13 and $18 per square foot respectively.

COMPANY INFORMATION
Northern Counties sends a brochure of floor plans and renderings with information on design and construction, their panelizing process, and particulars of their earth-sheltered design for $3. Several model homes are open seven days a week near the plant in Upperville.

PACIFIC MODERN HOMES, INC.
P.O. Box 670
Elk Grove, CA 95624
(916) 423-3150

PRODUCT RANGE
Pacific supplies over forty standard models ranging in size from 670 to 2,200 square feet. Stock plans include rustic chalet and barn style homes as well as typical California ranch-style houses. Nearly 50 percent of the firm's production is customized homes ranging to 4,000 square feet.

PREFAB COMPONENTS
Panelized walls are made up in 12-foot sections using Douglas fir structural timbers and ⅝-inch siding. All double-glazed windows are installed and trimmed. All roofing is shop-made trusses. The shell framing package consisting of a closed-in house arrives at the site with only metal-clad entry doors and double-glazed sliders (all pre-hung) unattached. Pacific provides two-stage delivery: first the shell, then, when you or your contractor is ready, the finishing package of cabinets, interior doors, shelving, trim, and more.

MATERIALS
Douglas fir 303 shiplap pattern siding is standard, but ⅜-inch CCX may be substituted, allowing stucco or wood plank finishing. Many builder or owner-builder options are available, including extra insulation, 2 x 6-inch framing, and solar heating systems.

SPECIAL FEATURES
Because panelized wall sections are shipped with many operations normally reserved for site work already completed, these homes can be erected even by inexperienced owner-builders. The firm estimates that 20 to 50 percent savings are possible when you buy largely prefinished pieces of a house.

RELATIVE SIZE/COST
Costs of the shell package (minus only roof shingles and garage door) plus second-stage delivery packages of finishing materials range from a low of $8 to roughly $13 per square foot.

COMPANY INFORMATION
Pacific Modern offers a full brochure of house plans with pictorial views and floor plans for $1. The firm sells predominantly through a series of licensed dealers in California, Nevada, Arizona, and Hawaii. Inquire about shipping to other sites. In business over fifteen years, Pacific has packaged over ten thousand panelized homes.

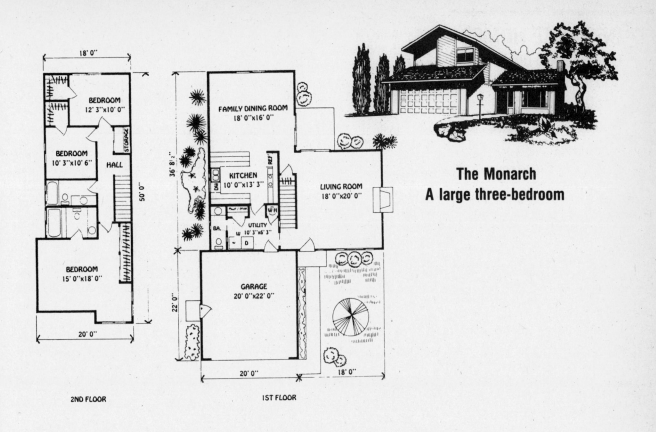

18' 0"

BEDROOM
12' 3"x10' 0"

BEDROOM
10' 3"x10' 6"

STORAGE

HALL

50' 0"

BEDROOM
15' 0"x18' 0"

20' 0"

2ND FLOOR

FAMILY DINING ROOM
18' 0"x16' 0"

36' 8' 2"

KITCHEN
10' 0"x13' 3"

REF

LIVING ROOM
18' 0"x20' 0"

W H

BA.

UTILITY
10' 3"x6' 3"

W
D

22' 0"

GARAGE
20' 0"x22' 0"

20' 0"

18' 0"

1ST FLOOR

**The Monarch
A large three-bedroom**

**The Trinity
four-bedroom house**

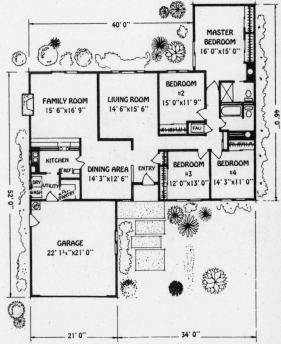

40' 0"

MASTER
BEDROOM
16' 0"x15' 0"

46' 0"

FAMILY ROOM
15' 6"x16' 9"

LIVING ROOM
14' 6"x15' 6"

BEDROOM
#2
15' 0"x11' 9"

FAU

KITCHEN

REF

DINING AREA
14' 3"x12' 6"

ENTRY

BEDROOM
#3
12' 0"x13' 0"

BEDROOM
#4
14' 3"x11' 0"

52' 0"

DRY
WASH

UTILITY

PANTRY

GARAGE
22' 1¾"x21' 0"

21' 0"

34' 0"

TRUE VALUE HOMES
6425 East Thomas
Scottsdale, AZ 85251
(602) 945-2773

PRODUCT RANGE
True Value makes fourteen standard models of homes and cabins, sold from sales offices in Scottsdale, Phoenix, and Verde Valley. The panelized homes may be erected by the company or owner-builders, and modified to suit individual needs. Sold in shell and complete kits, the homes range from 640 square feet to 2,200 square feet.

PREFAB COMPONENTS
True Value complete kits include 2 x 4 wall framing 16 inches on center, interior and exterior doors, finished roofing, exterior walls with Thermax board, insulation, plumbing and bath fixtures, cabinets, vanities, counters, floor tile, interior paneling and drywall, a 200-amp service, smoke detectors, hardware. Complete turnkey units include carpeting, painting, heating, and air conditioning.

MATERIALS
Standards include 1¾-inch hollow-core exterior doors, copper wiring, Wilson Art counters, one-piece tubs with ceramic tile surround, R-11 in walls and R-19 in ceilings. Special energy-saving packages include 2 x 6 wall studs 24 inches on center, R-19 wall insulation and R-30 in ceilings, double-glazed windows, and sliding glass doors.

SPECIAL FEATURES
True Value Homes are affiliated with the Ponderosa Lumber Company, which buys in bulk direct from lumber mills. The firm also manufactures its own roof trusses, prehung door units, and all wall component sections.

RELATIVE SIZE/COST
True Value serves the western United States and Hawaii, offering delivery in Arizona included in the home price. Typical costs for a 1,500-square-foot model are $15,000 for the shell kit, $24,000 for the complete kit, roughly $22,000 for the shell kit erected on site, and $33,000 for the complete package erected. The full turnkey package is roughly $48,000.

COMPANY INFORMATION
True Value serves the western states and Hawaii. The firm is a member of the NAHB.

The Suburban four-bedroom home

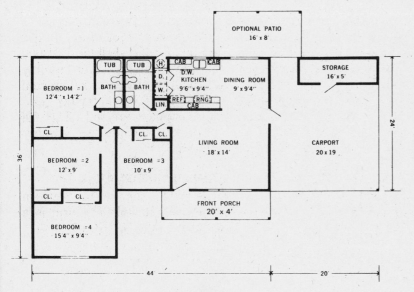

OPTIONAL PATIO
16' x 8'

| BEDROOM #1 | TUB | TUB | | CAB | CAB | | STORAGE |
| 12'4" x 14'2" | BATH | BATH | H | D.W. KITCHEN | DINING ROOM | | 16' x 5' |

BEDROOM #1
12'4" x 14'2"

TUB TUB
BATH BATH

H
D.
W.
LIN

CAB CAB
D.W.
KITCHEN
9'6" x 9'4"
REF RNG
CAB

DINING ROOM
9' x 9'4"

STORAGE
16' x 5'

CL.

CL. CL.

LIVING ROOM
18' x 14'

CARPORT
20 x 19

BEDROOM #2
12' x 9'

BEDROOM #3
10' x 9'

CL. CL.

BEDROOM #4
15'4" x 9'4"

FRONT PORCH
20' x 4'

36

24

44

20

The Esquire three-bedroom home

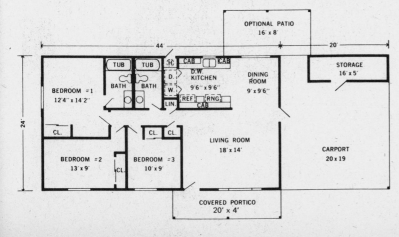

OPTIONAL PATIO
16' x 8'

44

20

BEDROOM #1
12'4" x 14'2"

TUB TUB
BATH BATH

H
D.
W.
LIN

CAB CAB
D.W.
KITCHEN
9'6" x 9'6"
REF RNG
CAB

DINING
ROOM
9' x 9'6"

STORAGE
16' x 5'

24

CL.

CL. CL.

LIVING ROOM
18' x 14'

CARPORT
20 x 19

BEDROOM #2
13' x 9'

BEDROOM #3
10' x 9'

CL.

COVERED PORTICO
20' x 4'

DOME HOMES

ALUMINUM GEODESIC SPHERES
4019 West Park Road
Hollywood, FL 33021
(305) 625-9436

PRODUCT RANGE
These unique aluminum frames are available in dome diameters up to 45 feet. The dome struts are lightweight aluminum, easily assembled with straight sections on hub connectors. The minimal designs have been used as pool enclosures, greenhouses, bubble shelters over parts of homes with a lot of uncovered outdoor spaces, and other shelters.

PREFAB COMPONENTS
A variety of dome packages are offered, including interlocking triangular frames, glazing panels, frame panels and more, depending on the dome diameter and design.

MATERIALS
Aluminum Geodesic's basic strut is made of roll-formed 1 x 1 hollow aluminum with built-in glazing groove. Struts are connected with arrow-shaped corner pieces and aluminum studs threaded for acorn nuts.

SPECIAL FEATURES
The dome struts are extremely lightweight, with slot grooves for easy assembly of glazing panels.

RELATIVE SIZE/COST
Although these domes are sold more as enclosures than houses, even as attention-getters for retail stores, Aluminum Geodesic is one of the very few firms selling geodesics in full spheres, and with minimal framing. Sphere fractions with glazing can make partial or full rooftop bubbles, and serve as the roof section of custom sunrooms. Costs are quoted on request.

COMPANY INFORMATION
A set of plans and a sphere kit are sent for $20, a bit steep for a look. Try writing the firm for basic information first.

DAYSTAR SHELTER CORP.

22509 Cedar Drive
Bethel, MN 55005
(612) 753-4981

PRODUCT RANGE

Daystar offers over thirty dome kits in low-, mid-, and high-profile designs. These differ in the placement of the imaginary line through a complete dome sphere where the structure meets the foundation. The 26-foot-diameter Brahms series (they are all named after composers—quite a relief after the endless permutations of Woodland and Woodcrest and Woodridge) begins an increase in diameters up to 49-foot domes with about 3,000 square feet of usable floor space on two levels. Daystar also makes 55- and up to 80-foot-diameter domes (the Grieg), truly gigantic interior spaces normally reserved for commercial applications. The firm also produces custom plans.

PREFAB COMPONENTS

Daystar sells closed-in-frame packages, and complete interior packages. Their shell includes all precut exterior panels, color-coded hub connectors for structural components, insulation and vapor barrier, ½-inch triangular cover panels and trim, custom windows, doors, panelized AWWF sections, first-floor frame, siding, and shingles. Acknowledging the peculiarities of interior finishing in a dome—a lot of angles that will be unfamiliar to most owner-builders—Daystar interior packages include all wallboard and trim, stairs, closets, cabinets, finished floor, plus complete mechanical systems: heating, plumbing, and wiring.

MATERIALS

Daystar domes are built with highly engineered plywood beams; 2 x 16-inch assemblies of solid plywood panels set into grooves in dimensional timbers top and bottom. Simple triangular construction without a typical maze of 2 x 4 or 2 x 6 struts filling the geodesic frame permits the use of precut, triangular, 12-inch-thick fiber glass batts, and quick installation of building skins. Interior sheathing is ½-inch chipboard panels. Operating custom windows are aluminum-clad and double-glazed. Exterior siding below fiber glass–shingled roof sections is textured fir plywood. Remember that only the lower, vertical sections of a dome are treated with wall siding. Much of the facade is steeply angled roofing, and takes shingles. Many material options are available—for example, cedar shake roofing, and t&g pine or cedar interior planking.

SPECIAL FEATURES

Daystar offers an unusual, slightly raised cupola for ventilation at the top of their domes, and a version raised enough above the geodesic roofline for operable vent windows and a nice view.

RELATIVE SIZE/COST

Daystar's 26-foot-diameter, mid-profile dome with 475 square feet on both basement and first floor, plus 150 feet of usable loft space (1,100 square feet total), is roughly $4,700 for shell only, $17,000 for complete exterior package, $27,000 for interior and exterior packages combined—$4, $15, and $24 per square foot respectively. The Copland model, a high-profile, 42-foot-diameter dome, has 1,270 square feet on both basement and first-floor levels, plus 935 feet of usable second-story space (3,475 square feet total). The dome shell is $16,000, the exterior package $42,000, the combination package $66,000; $4.50, $12.00, and $19.00 per square foot respectively.

COMPANY INFORMATION

Daystar offers construction supervision for owner-builders, and periodic two-day seminars covering dome construction, also design and financing, capped by a tour of several dome homes. A brief flier sent on request includes information on ½-inch to 1-foot scale-model frame kits—a great way to preview your home. A full-color catalog with costs and specifications is $8.

DOME CREATIONS
211 E. Maulding
Las Vegas, NV 89119
(702) 387-6311

PRODUCT RANGE
Dome Creations has an extensive line of dome kits in 26- to 50-foot diameters, and several profiles (³⁄₈, ½, or ⁵⁄₈ sphere segments), also garage kits, precut dormers, dome extensions, riser walls, prefabricated wood foundations, skylights, and cupolas. Square footage ranges from 700 to 3,000 over two stories.

PREFAB COMPONENTS
Dome Creations offers owner-builder kits and completely finished turnkey houses. Typical packages include either 2 x 4 or 2 x 6 shell struts, hardware, exterior and interior sheathing, skylights, insulation, counters and cabinets, carpeting and tile, even smoke detectors.

MATERIALS
Exterior sheathing is ½ inch CDX over #1 grade 2 x 4 construction or #2 and better 2 x 6 construction. Interior sheathing is waferboard glued and stapled to the frame. A wide selection of options include hardwood cabinet finish, various types of siding and roof finishes. Extra-cost options include garage, fireplace, ceramic tile, shake roof, and exterior decks.

SPECIAL FEATURES
Dome Creations can alter designs for extreme wind or snow loads. Their trapezoid wall units can be assembled with siding, windows, and doors to speed assembly time. The firm estimates that their domes can be raised and locked in one day.

RELATIVE SIZE/COST
The firm's smallest dome, a 26-foot diameter with 735 square feet on two levels is roughly $4,500 with 2 x 4 framing, and $5,500 with 2 x 6 framing. The largest unit, a 50-foot diameter with 1,800 square feet on the first floor and 1,100 on the second level is roughly $13,000 in 2 x 6 framing. Their Delta IV model, a 45-foot diameter dome, ³⁄₈ sphere section with 2,000 square feet on two levels is $57,000. That's the turnkey price, less land, ready to run.

COMPANY INFORMATION
Dome Creations, a member of the National Dome Council, has offices in Las Vegas and has built extensively with treated wood foundations in the southwest. The firm offers good literature on that little-known foundation system.

DOME CREATIONS (continued)

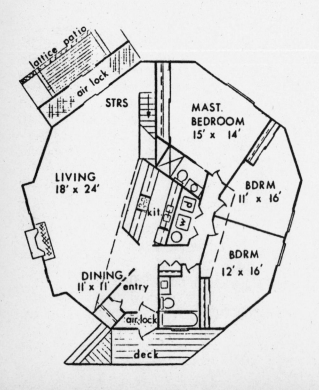

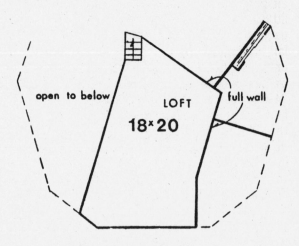

The Delta IV ⅜ sphere dome

DOMES AMERICA
6 S. 771 Western Avenue
Clarendon Hills, IL 60514
(312) 986-5060

PRODUCT RANGE
Domes America makes a wide range of ⅜- and ⅝-fraction domes, including homes, stores, an airport terminal, office complexes of clustered domes, and churches. The different fractions mean that either a little more than half or a little less than half of a complete geodesic sphere is framed. The larger fraction nets greatly increased interior volume. Both fraction models are available from 24-foot diameters with 13-foot-3-inch peaks and 486 square feet on the first-floor level, to 65-foot-diameter domes with 26-foot-5-inch peaks and 3,682 square feet. In ⅜-fraction models additional diameters of 75, 90, and 120 feet are available. The largest model has a 48-foot-8-inch peak and nearly 11,000 square feet on the first-floor level.

PREFAB COMPONENTS
The Domes America dealer network provides review of architectural plans, supervision of foundation layout (over full basement, crawl space, slab, piers, and other options), erection of the dome shell, and supervision of roofing application. Finishing is left to the owner-builder or contractor.

MATERIALS
Domes America makes panelized buildings. Triangular sections are fabricated with 2 x 4 or 2 x 6 framing members and ½-inch CDX plywood. These stress-skin prefab panels are glued and bolted together to form precise pentagons or hexagons. These major sections are then set by crane, although all models except the largest domes can be set by hand in about eight hours. Diameters over 55 feet are always set by crane, also in roughly eight hours. The firm manufactures its own skylights, using double-glazed bronzed acrylic with a ¾-inch dead-air layer. Among several materials options are special-order ⅜-fraction domes prepared for pool enclosures.

SPECIAL FEATURES
The firm offers custom architectural design, also full architectural review by a committee of professionals who check plans for economy, energy efficiency, code compliance, etc. More than two thirds of Domes America homes are completely built by their dealers. The rest are finished by owner-builders.

RELATIVE SIZE/COST
Domes America's ⅜-fraction, 24-foot-diameter package providing 486 square feet, with two 4-foot hex skylights and a 42-inch riser wall, is roughly $8,000 FOB Chicago. A ⅝-fraction, 39-foot-diameter model with 1,238 square feet available on the first floor, 1,156 on the second, and another 500 on the third (the peak is over 23 feet), including five hex skylights, is roughly $15,500 FOB Chicago.

COMPANY INFORMATION
The firm provides representative floor plans on request. They enclose an interesting graphic comparison of dome homes and conventional living space.

DOMICILES, INC.
Route 1
Numa, IA 52575
(515) 437-4723

PRODUCT RANGE

Domiciles manufactures dome shells from 26- to 45-foot diameters. Most are half-fraction spheres, or half of the total dome shape. The company literature points out that this shape makes the most efficient use of dome space, and lets the dome superstructure rest flat on the foundation sill, whereas some fraction domes rest on beveled sills and produce an outward thrust force on the foundation wall. Domicile estimates that their 26-foot-diameter model provides 467 square feet on the first floor with 267 square feet of loft space. Their 45-foot-diameter model has 1,490 feet on the first floor, 1,347 on the second, 700 on the third-floor loft, totaling over 3,500 square feet.

PREFAB COMPONENTS

Domiciles' kit includes all steel frame connectors, precut wood struts, a set of one-piece triangular exterior panels, a similar set for inside, furring strips for vapor barrier and panel mounting, a framed 24-inch riser wall, plus adhesive sealant for exterior panel installation. Kit options include gray, bronze, or clear glazing in circles, trapezoids, and triangles, precut pine interior trim, and a special garage door and overhang dormer kit for their 26-foot model.

MATERIALS

The dome framework is construction-grade timber, 2 x 6 Douglas fir, used with furring strips set as interior purlins to allow a continuous insulation blanket across framing bays and structural members. The precut, triangular, one-piece closing panels are waferboard stock, sealed and glued on all exterior seams.

SPECIAL FEATURES

Domiciles offers an interesting comparison chart showing the thermal performance of their glued and sealed panel system with various types of insulation. While some housing standards predict 35 percent air infiltration, Domicile's double waferboard with fiber glass insulation and vapor barrier produces virtually no infiltration and an R-23.

RELATIVE SIZE/COST

Domiciles' shell kits for 26-foot-diameter half-fraction domes cost roughly $6,000, about $8 per square foot. The 45-foot model is roughly $17,000, about $5 per square foot for usable floor space on three stories.

COMPANY INFORMATION

Domicile's information kit is sent for $2. The firm can provide design and construction services, and is equipped to design in passive and active solar systems.

GEODESIC DOMES, INC.

10290 Davison Road
Davison, MI 48423
(313) 653-2383

PRODUCT RANGE

Geodesic makes $3/8$ and $5/8$ sphere section domes in 30-, 35-, 39-, and 45-foot diameters, and a small 26-foot model with a 200-square-foot sleeping loft. Extensions are sold in 2-foot increments, so that it is possible to create entryways, extra rooms, even connecting rooms between domes, all within the modular system of construction.

PREFAB COMPONENTS

Basic kit packages include sixty prefabricated and predrilled panels with sheathing attached, all fasteners and hardware, five sets of canopy systems to protect window and door openings, riser wall materials (optional on the 39- and 45-foot models), insulating foam sill sealer, and all temporary bracing required during assembly. The $5/8$ section domes are shipped in ninety panels.

MATERIALS

Geodesic's panels are made with exterior sheathing composed of Aspen wafers bonded into a seamless waterproof panel. The assembly is made with natural resins that do not contain formaldehyde. Skylights are double acrylic, bronze tinted with bronze frames. Finishing materials are not included.

SPECIAL FEATURES

Geodesic can provide interesting plans for double domes, triple domes arranged in a V-pattern and arc pattern. The firm also offers an interesting Dutch dormer, which is a hooded minidormer generally placed above rain shedding extensions over first-floor openings.

RELATIVE SIZE/COST

Geodesic's Sierra series with a 2-foot riser wall is roughly $6,500 for the basic package, with options for dormers ($300), cupola ($750), and 4-foot extensions ($500). For 2 x 6 framing roughly 15 percent is added to the basic package cost.

COMPANY INFORMATION

Geodesic ships from two factories and can provide on-site supervision by a factory-trained assembly expert. Both plants are open to the public and have erected model homes on display. Write to arrange a visit.

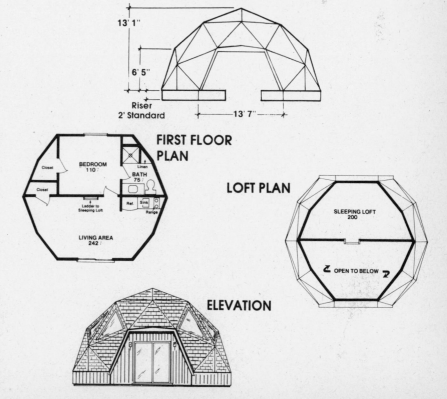

The Alpine 26 foot dome

13' 1"

6' 5"

Riser
2' Standard

13' 7"

FIRST FLOOR PLAN

Closet
BEDROOM
110
Linen
BATH
75
Closet
Ladder to
Sleeping Loft
Ref. Sink
Range
LIVING AREA
242

LOFT PLAN

SLEEPING LOFT
200

OPEN TO BELOW

ELEVATION

GEODESIC HOMES
P.O. Box 1675
Bailey, CO 80421
(303) 838-5345

PRODUCT RANGE
Geodesic offers a series of domes up to a 39-foot-diameter model with 1,100 square feet on the first floor and 12,000 cubic feet of interior space. The company makes full-house enclosures and canopy domes with strut supports used as carports and open-sided shelters.

PREFAB COMPONENTS
Packages from Geodesic can be assembled to include completely panelized frame sections. The factory-built panels have 2 x 4 framing with exterior plywood ready for shingling. The kit includes triangular space frames, base plates predrilled for anchor bolts, machine bolts with washers and nuts for panel assembly. Five types of openings are ordered independently, including prefab door and window combination panels, patio glass doors, and doors with triangular glass-panel extension wings.

MATERIALS
Base plates and framing are 2 x 4 Douglas fir or western hemlock. Stress-skin panels are $3/8$-inch Duraply exterior-grade Douglas fir plywood with medium-density plastic overlay. Hardware includes $3/8$ x 4-inch hex head machine bolts, 8-inch anchors, and 18-gauge steel strapping. Openings can be ordered in $3/16$-inch sheet glass or $5/8$-inch insulated glass.

SPECIAL FEATURES
The firm recommends erection over slab foundations with a base riser wall of 12 to 16 inches. The firm provides engineering drawings, and a form jig to use with slab construction.

RELATIVE SIZE/COST
The 26-foot-diameter dome with 500 square feet is around $4,500, or $9 per square foot. Larger models with 1,100 square feet and a 39-foot-diameter (enough room for kitchen, dining room, living room, den, three beds, and two baths) are around $7,500, or $7 per square foot.

COMPANY INFORMATION
Geodesic supplies spec sheets of sample models on request, including shell costs, materials lists, typical floor plans, and a photo of the finished product.

MONTEREY DOMES

1760 Chicago Avenue
Box 55116
Riverside, CA 92517
(714) 684-2601

PRODUCT RANGE

Monterey is one of the largest established dome companies in the industry. They offer eleven different models and sizes ranging from less than 300 square feet in a 20-foot-diameter dome to over 3,200 square feet in a 45-foot-diameter model. With five eighths or three eighths of the total sphere included, Monterey produces thirty-six standardized plans, including a basic one-room cabin and a 4,000-square-foot, four-bedroom, two-and-a-half-bath cluster. Domes of equal or unequal diameters may be clustered (pictured) for a nearly limitless number of designs.

PREFAB COMPONENTS

All of the Monterey kit parts are precut, predrilled, and color-coded for easy assembly around their patented hub and strut hardware system. Marketing manager Richard Bendix writes, "The assembly system makes building a dome simple even for the novice builder. Plus our fully illustrated Assembly Manual takes the owner through the building process in a step-by-step fashion." The kits include hub connectors, struts and studs, shell plywood, hardware and nails, base walls, blueprints, and construction manuals.

MATERIALS

Wood framing is all precut Douglas fir graded #1 and kiln-dried for stability. Plywood sheathing is ½-inch CC exterior. All nails and bolts come with 5 percentage overage—in case you're sloppy and drop a bunch of them into the concrete footings. Monterey's foundation package consists of a 2 x 4 kiln-dried studwall with pressure-treated sills and exterior-grade ½-inch sheathing. The company also has opening extension frames (the dome version of a first-floor dormer, designed to provide wide access) and numerous triangular and five-sided skylights.

SPECIAL FEATURES

Monterey can provide custom design services. They have also developed an interesting roof system of preformed triangular panels that conform to the dome surface, with simulated shake patterns formed into the panel.

RELATIVE SIZE/COST

Kit prices start at $4,000 for the smallest dome shell kit. The large, ⅝-fraction, 45-foot-diameter Alpine model is about $15,000. Monterey's ongoing survey of customers shows that finished costs range between $24 and $30 per square foot. Monterey sells com-

plete sets of working drawings, series of five interlocked flat-plate solar collectors, and framed-in packages for skylights and for dormers.

COMPANY INFORMATION
Monterey offers a massive amount of consumer information in a kit for $6. It includes a 100-page color catalog and plans book, a specifications guide, and information on materials and construction. The firm has regional offices serving all areas of the country. Monterey is a member of the National Dome Council of the National Association of Home Builders.

NATURAL SPACES, INC.

Route 3
North Branch, MN 55056
(612) 674-4292

PRODUCT RANGE

Natural Spaces is an interesting dome firm offering a wide selection of sizes and configurations, also some very innovative applications—earth-sheltered domes, for example. Basic models include ten plans from 485 to 5,500 square feet (from 26- to 49-foot diameters in low-, mid-, and high-profile elevations). The firm also makes up to 80-foot diameter domes. In addition to earth-sheltered designs, the company offers an extensive array of window designs and domes mated to AWWF foundation systems.

PREFAB COMPONENTS

Natural Spaces offers the full range of prefab options: a hub hardware connector system, pre-cut exterior shell, fully finished exterior, even delivery and set-up by factory crews so you can participate as much or as little as you want.

MATERIALS

A unique hub system uses strut hardware with a protruding tongue that is locked into the hub with a wedged pin. 2 x 6 struts require no angle cutting, and are pinned into the hardware sleeves with ½-inch bolts. Typical systems have ½-inch interior ply dimensional timber struts, and ¾-inch exterior ply. However, up to 24-inch-deep double struts can provide up to a 22-inch wall with an R-64 rating for cold climate sites. Interior ply is waferboard. Exterior ply is ¾-inch tongue and groove. The firm's unique earth-sheltered design is rated to hold 18 to 24 inches of earth over treated foundation-grade plywood. Insulated windows consist of two, three, or even four panes of glass.

SPECIAL FEATURES

Natural Spaces offers two special services. First is a completely furnished dome in North Carolina (possibly the first of several) that may be rented by prospective buyers for a few days or a week to actually "test" the dome for a modest fee before buying. A novel idea. Also, the firm runs an owner-builder dome school in North Branch (about 50 miles from Min-

neapolis) offering intensive two-day "hands-on" instruction.

RELATIVE SIZE/COST

A 26-foot-diameter model ranging from 485 to 1,100 square feet depending on profile and layout is roughly $1,300 for the hub system, $4,000 for the precut shell package, and $14,000 for the finished exterior dome package. A large 40-foot-diameter model with 1,250 to 4,000 square feet depending on configuration is roughly $3,500 for the hub system, $10,000 for the shell, and $30,000 for the finished exterior dome. Natural Spaces comprehensive information materials package is available for $12, including a full plan portfolio and an extensive guide to dome design, construction, energy use, and more.

COMPANY INFORMATION

Natural Spaces provides comprehensive information on construction, financing, and energy costs. The firm's principals are members of the Minnesota Society of the American Institute of Architects, the American Underground Space Association, and the Dome Association.

The Model 625 mid-profile 29 foot dome The version on the left is 1,650 square feet; the one on the right is 2,025 square feet.

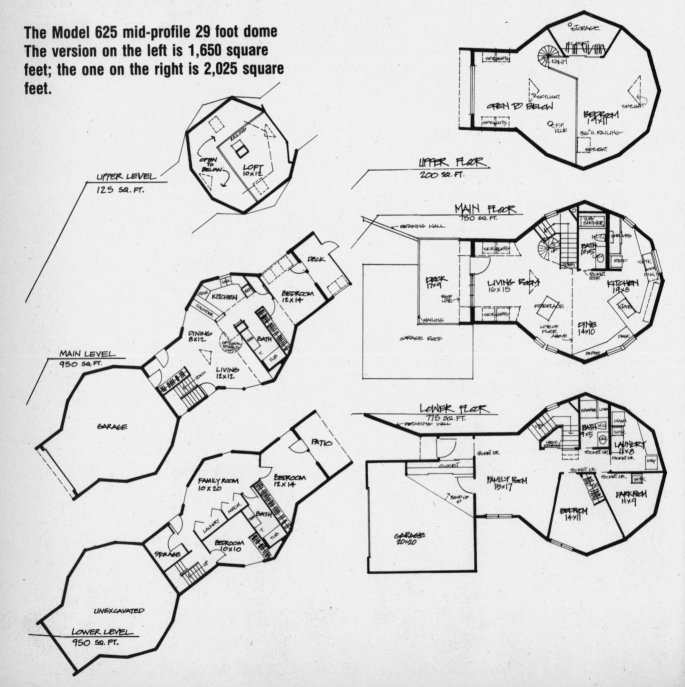

TIMBERLINE GEODESICS, INC.
2015 Blake Street
Berkeley, CA 94704
(415) 849-4481

PRODUCT RANGE
Timberline makes twelve different basic domes, from 18- to 45-foot diameters. Six diameters are available as 3/8- or 5/8-sphere fractions. (See Glossary for an explanation of fraction domes.) Eight different dome packages are available for each variety, which gives you about 100 different choices just from stock plans, so you can choose how much material you want to buy locally and cut on the job.

PREFAB COMPONENTS
For do-it-yourselfers, the company offers a connector-only package with cutting and assembly plans. The heavy-duty steel hub connectors (tested to failure under 12,000-pound loads) have predrilled flanges for bolt connections to the wood frame. The firm's complete kit also includes precut plywood sheathing.

MATERIALS
Timberline's struts and studs are 2 x 6-dimensional Hem-Fir or Douglas fir. Plywood is ½-inch CDX, color-coded to match struts and blocking. Riser walls used to lift the sphere off the ground (precut walls up to 8 feet are available) are also 2 x 6 framing 16 inches on center. Timberline also makes triangular double-glazed acrylic skylights.

SPECIAL FEATURES
In addition to ventilating cupolas, dormer frames, and such, Timberline offers specialty hardware called ledger hangers. Even when owner-builders buy precut sheathing, they are often hit by a theoretical barrier where geodesic shapes must be translated to conventional linear framing—for example, where second-floor joists meet the faceted dome frame. The ledger hanger fits into the strut hardware, bridging the theoretical gap, and allowing easy drop-in-and-bolt transitions to 2 x 10 ledgers from which joists are suspended.

RELATIVE SIZE/COST
An 18-foot, 3/8-section sphere is roughly $4,500 for the complete kit, $3,500 for struts and connectors only. Timberline's largest dome, a 45-foot-diameter 5/8-section sphere, is roughly $12,000 for the complete kit, and $9,000 for struts and connectors.

COMPANY INFORMATION
Timberline provides very thorough information on request, including a detailed, step-by-step planning sequence making clear exactly what components you need for different dome configurations. Although so many different kit package choices may seem confusing, the variety represents a realistic approach by the company, accommodating skilled do-it-yourselfers, novices, and owners who hire contractors to handle construction.

TIMBER-WALL HOMES

CEDAR FOREST PRODUCTS CO.

107 W. Colden Street
Polo, IL 61064
(815) 946-3994

PRODUCT RANGE

Cedar Forest makes an extensive line of solid cedar homes, and outbuildings such as gazebos and octagonal shelters. The rugged but clean-lined homes range from simple, two-room "sportsman" cabins to elaborate multistory homes.

PREFAB COMPONENTS

Standard models include solid wall timbers, 10-inch securing spikes, sealants and caulking, partition walls of Douglas fir studs with cedar paneling, structural and finished roofing with CDX ½-inch sheathing, steel-clad exterior doors, solid-core luan (a species of mahogany) interior doors, double-hung windows—a complete, closed-in house.

MATERIALS

Solid western red cedar walls are made of five cedar planks laminated into 5 x 8-inch timbers with double tongue and groove locking between courses. The timbers are built up layer by layer. Butt joints in walls are also tongue and groove, providing a five-ply overlap against the weather. Corners are locked up with a mortised dovetail pattern. The precut cedar timbers are predrilled for 10-inch spikes at 5-foot intervals. All wall timbers are stabilized by kiln drying to 12 percent moisture content.

SPECIAL FEATURES

Innovative owner-builders and designers should note that this company manufactures a great many recreational buildings using massive, built-up cedar rafters and arches to span vast areas without posts or partition walls. For example, their low-pitch cedar-beam shelters in stock, precut sizes up to 50 by 76 feet (that's quite a room) are easily adapted to closed-in living space, allowing any arrangement of interior partitions.

RELATIVE SIZE/COST

Quoted on inquiry.

COMPANY INFORMATION

Cedar Forest Products ships nationally, although most of their sales are east of the Rocky Moun-

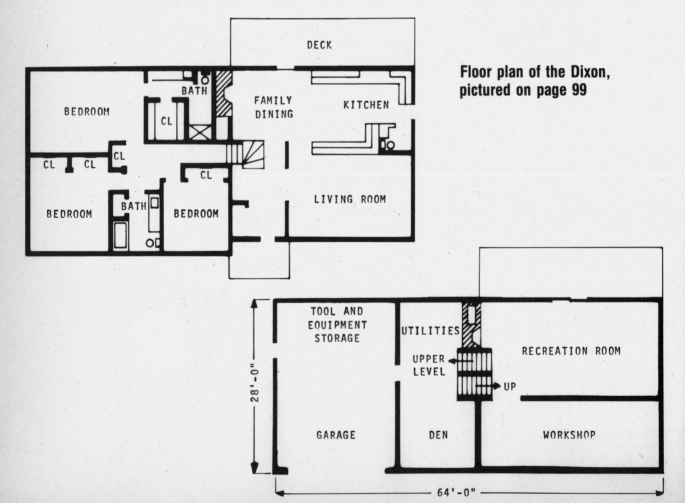

Floor plan of the Dixon, pictured on page 99

tains. The firm is a member of the National Recreation & Parks Association, American Camping Association, and National Lumber and Building Materials Dealers Association. In addition to brochures showing floor plans and pictorial views of many homes, ask for catalog 1084, covering park, camp, and recreation buildings. Not many companies offer such an array of clean-cut, utilitarian, but elegant clear-span structures. Clear spans in conventional housing are limited by the performance characteristics of conventional timbers, commonly to roughly 20 feet, and even then only with some high-class carpentry. The prefab alternative pays off again here, offering exceptional space framed by preengineered, precut timbers.

JUSTUS LOG HOMES
P.O. Box 24426
4300 South 104th Place
Seattle, WA 98124
(206) 721-5630

PRODUCT RANGE
Although Justus offers many standard floor plans, all kinds of modifications are possible, so that most of the company's homes are largely custom products. The basic design is called a prow, describing the forward-sweeping roof line and gentle V-shape to the "forward" wall of the main room, which has large glazing panels protected by a liberal overhang. These solid cedar wall homes range from under 1,000- to over 3,000-square-foot stock plans.

PREFAB COMPONENTS
Justus homes are built around solid, kiln-dried western red cedar walls, including windows, fixed glazing, precut trim, cedar shakes, stair assemblies, decks and balconies with railings, and insulation—everything needed to close in the cedar shell. Several alternate packages are available.

MATERIALS
Justus timbers are kiln-dried, solid 3- and 4-inch cedar. The stabilized timbers can be friction fitted in the field. Also, they are lighter, and easier to handle. Justus timbers are not butted in the wall, but are overlapped with an interlocking joint to eliminate potential air infiltration. All types of specially insulated glazing panels and rigid insulating roof decks are available—even double timber walls, R-40 walls, and R-50 roofs.

SPECIAL FEATURES
To put you in the right mood, Justus has impregnated a patch of the catalog with cedar essence, so that as you leaf through the various floor plans and read about the solid timber walls, you are surrounded by the scent of a cedar forest. There are quality carpentry details throughout, and one outstanding feature is the Justus partition wall system. Where timber walls are used inside the house and butt at right angles to the exterior walls, stable, kiln-dried timbers permit a dovetail joint—a channel cut into the exterior wall into which dovetail "keys" of the partition timbers are inserted.

RELATIVE SIZE/COST
The Justus Alpental, a chalet-type home with 1,646 square feet, is roughly $26,000; $16 per square foot. Their large Cascade model with 3,346 square feet is roughly $41,000; $12 per square foot.

COMPANY INFORMATION
Justus sells through a dealer network, and has model home centers in Tacoma, Seattle, and British Columbia. The aromatic planning and design information package is sent for $5.

PAN ABODE CEDAR HOMES

4350 Lake Washington
Boulevard N
Renton, WA 98055
(206) 255-8260

PRODUCT RANGE

Pan Abode offers thirty-five models of elegant solid cedar wall homes, from a 350-square-foot cabin called the Eagle's Nest through a wide range of homes of 1,000 to 2,000 square feet and up to models over 3,000 square feet. The patented, interlocked timber walls with notched, overlapped corners present clean-lined, contemporary designs, sweeping roof lines, and large clear-span interior spaces. Pan Abode offers 3- or 4-inch-thick cedar walls, an incredible double wall with insulating cavity for an R-40 cold-climate rating, and combinations with stick-frame and paneled interior partitions.

PREFAB COMPONENTS

Home packages include Hem-Fir floor joists and ⅝-inch CDX decking; 3 x 6-inch or 4 x 6-inch western red cedar timber walls—all precut, tongue and grooved, with locking corners, labeled and wrapped—roof beams, all roofing, windows, doors, trim, insulation, and hardware and sealants required for a closed-in home with partition walls. Many options are available, and over 90 percent of Pan Abode's standard plans are modified in one way or another to suit owner's needs. About 50 percent are assembled by owner-builders.

MATERIALS

The Pan Abode system of tongue and groove locking walls was patented in 1955 by Aage Jensen, a Danish cabinetmaker who started the company. The western red cedar is all old growth, tight knot, and air-dried. Exposed roof decking is 2 x 6 t&g kiln-dried hemlock over massive 4 x 12 Douglas fir beams. Homes over 1,000 square feet have solid cedar prehung doors and cedar trim. Roof insulation is an interesting sandwich of 4-inch rigid foam with two layers of ½-inch CDX plywood netting R-38. Pan Abode also offers quality details, including Cabot's Stain Wax on kitchen cabinets, and Schlage locks.

SPECIAL FEATURES

Because of the simplified wall construction, where interlocking timbers provide finished interior and exterior surfaces, insulating value (and mass gain benefits), and structural support, several conventional steps of construction are eliminated. Pan Abode president John L. Hubbard says that a crew of three working with utility system subcontractors can complete a 2,000-square-foot house in sixty days.

RELATIVE SIZE/COST

A small, 975-square-foot chalet is roughly $25,000 with 4 x 6 solid walls, $30,000 with massive double walls and insulating core; $25 and $30 per square foot respectively. The schooner model pictured, with 2,365 square feet, is roughly $66,000 with 3 x 6 walls, $71,000 with 4 x 6 walls, and $76,000 with double walls; $28, $30, and $32 per square foot respectively.

COMPANY INFORMATION

Pan Abode offers a large package of information for $14.00, including a detailed construction guide and financing guide ($4.00 if purchased separately), solar energy guide ($2.50), and a stunning, full-color, thirty-six-page planning guide ($10.00) with countless pictures of Pan Abode homes on some breathtaking sites. A basic color brochure is sent on request.

PRE-CUT INTERNATIONAL HOMES, INC.

P.O. Box 886
Woodinville, WA 98072
(206) 668-8511

PRODUCT RANGE

International offers nearly fifty standard plans of completely pre-cut, solid laminated timber wall homes, including a 272-square-foot cabin, several small vacation homes under 1,000 square feet, and a wide range of larger homes up to 3,500 square feet. The firm has recently introduced a new se-ries of eight somewhat less contemporary-looking designs, featuring sweeping roof lines and dramatic glazing.

PREFAB COMPONENTS

International packages include laminated solid cedar walls, and a 4⅜-inch-thick alternative with ei-ther a 1½-inch polystyrene or po-lyurethane foam core. The com-plete weather shell includes double-glazed doors and windows, interior and exterior doors, joists and subflooring, and roofing, in-cluding insulation and cedar shakes. As is customary with many precut firms, the owner pre-pares a foundation and installs me-chanical systems.

MATERIALS

International makes three wall systems: a 2¾-inch three-piece lamination (offset to create tongue and groove locking) in cedar or pine, a 3 9/16-inch five-ply lamina-tion with double tongue and groove, and a 4⅜-inch five-ply wall with a 1½-inch insulating core. Concealed floor framing is 2 x 10 Hem-Fir with ¾-inch t&g plywood subfloor. Open-beamed ceilings are decked with 2 x 6 t&g planks covered with 2-inch polyurethane board, 15-pound felt paper, shake liner, and hand-split cedar shakes.

SPECIAL FEATURES

The firm offers a free cost esti-mate of any modification to their designs, which amounts to a free quote for a custom home using the International system of solid walls and T-joints against air infiltration.

RELATIVE SIZE/COST

The small 484-square-foot Saw-

dust package is roughly $17,500 in standard cedar ($36 per square foot), $15,500 in pine ($32 per square foot), $22,500 in foam-core cedar ($47 per square foot). An 1,844-square-foot contemporary-styled Glenwood model is roughly $48,000 in cedar, $42,000 in pine, and $57 in foam-core cedar; $26, $23, and $31 per square foot respectively.

COMPANY INFORMATION
A complete color presentation with floor plans and pictorial views of all models, plus information on options, materials, and construction, is sent for $5. Roughly 80 percent of International's customers participate in construction. The firm, in business since 1966, distributes homes throughout the United States, the Caribbean, Japan, and Australia.

EARTH-SHELTERED HOMES

TERRA-DOME CORP.
14 Oak Hill Cluster
Independence, MO 64050
(816) 229-6000

PRODUCT RANGE
Terra-Dome uses a highly engineered form system to fabricate modular concrete structures on site. The 24 x 24-foot and 28 x 28-foot vaults can be arranged in many configurations. For earth-sheltered homes, a typical plan has a large central vault with smaller vaults connected at each side, earth-sheltered on three sides (plus the roof), with large glazing areas to one exposure.

MATERIALS
The reinforced concrete domes have great strength due to the materials used and the inherent strength of vault design. The gently domed roof withstands twenty times the load design of conventional, flat-deck, earth-shelter homes. The company regularly runs over thirty tons of heavy earth-moving equipment over the domes during construction. Terra-Dome uses an ACI-recommended mix of 3,500 psi concrete with 3 percent entrained air. The firm is now testing a 6-inch-thick system with an integral steel fiber to replace their 10-inch-thick walls.

SPECIAL FEATURES
The unique dome shape allows a great degree of earth sheltering. Where many plans have only 2 feet of earth above the roof, Terra-Dome ceilings can support 8 feet plus the bulldozer to do the grading work. Although 2 feet of embedment offers substantial energy savings, year-round soil temperatures 8 feet below grade are extremely moderate, and in most locations vary only marginally year round. With effective glazing and site orientation, you can realistically expect to cut heating and cooling costs by 60 to 90 percent.

RELATIVE SIZE/COST
Costs are based on an owner-prepared site (excavation, footings, and 4 to 6 inches of crushed rock at ground level) at roughly $38 per yard of concrete. Terra-Dome's basic models plus complete waterproofing are roughly $10,000 for 24-foot domes and $13,000 for 28-foot models. Half-dome sections are also available, at half the cost.

COMPANY INFORMATION
Terra-Dome offers a plan and design service (for a $200 deposit they will initiate blueprints), and a

network of dealers familiar with the specialized on-site form system of construction. Basic literature is sent on request. A book of thirty-five floor plans with construction details, pictorial views, and more, called "Underground Design for the Twenty-first Century," is available for $5.75. A twenty-slide series on Terra-Dome homes is $6, and an interesting way to see what you'll get.

GREENHOUSES

GARDEN WAY SUNROOM/SOLAR GREENHOUSE

Ferry Road
Charlotte, VT 05445
(800) 343-1908

PRODUCT RANGE

Garden Way, best known for its Garden Way Cart (the big box on bicycle tires advertised everywhere), makes log splitters, rototillers, and more, plus a precut, panelized sun-room system with a complete line of solar components, designed for easy assembly on an owner-prepared foundation. The component system is 10 feet deep with a minimum length of 12 feet, extended in 4-foot sections. The largest installation so far is 68 feet long.

PREFAB COMPONENTS

The Garden Way system is built around arched laminated beams, all precut and sealed. Glazing is a sealed sandwich of two panes resting on an elastic gasket, angled at 60 degrees for maximum heat collection. Roof sections are $7/16$-inch exterior sheathing outside and $3/4$-inch paintable MDO plywood inside, wrapping a $3\frac{1}{2}$-inch rigid polyurethane core. Components include frames, sidewalls, glazing, an automatic heat transfer system to dump accumulated heat into connecting living spaces at predetermined temperatures, ventilators, plus a selection of doors and windows for the end walls.

MATERIALS

Packages are put together in modules. Several energy-efficient materials are available, such as a night insulating system of telescoping shutters covered with vinyl, weatherstripped into a grooved track in the laminated beams. The shutters provide an R-6.3 glazed wall. A series of fiber glass screens mounted outside are used as a summer sun block.

SPECIAL FEATURES

Garden Way offers thorough installation manuals and a twenty-four-hour hot line to help customers with the questions that inevitably arise during construction. Special financing plans are available, with no down payment.

RELATIVE SIZE/COST

Closed-in units shipped with two end walls cost approximately $6,500 for 10 x 12-foot units, $8,500 for 10 x 20 feet, and $12,000 for 10 x 32. Left and right end walls are included. You select either a lockable door or an awning window in each wall.

COMPANY INFORMATION

Garden Way sends their complete information kit for $3. It includes details of all solar options for the basic sun-room, including mass storage, clear wall, water-filled tubes, and an interesting booklet on solar orientation.

LORD & BURNHAM, DIVISION BURNHAM CORP.

Box 255
Irvington, NY 10533
(914) 591-8800

PRODUCT RANGE

Lord & Burnham has been manufacturing greenhouse and other glass enclosures since 1856. They offer an extensive series of freestanding greenhouses, solariums, wall enclosures, modules (with and without gable ends, with extended roof glazing), and prefab window greenhouses, all with single or double glazing. Most units are available in several styles—angled or vertical walls, rounded or curved eaves, with glazing down to the sill or to a riser wall sill. Models are sold in various standard widths, and with any number of modules to build a glazing wall as long as required. The firm also carries all types of greenhouse accessories, shelving, mechanical equipment, shading systems, etc.

PREFAB COMPONENTS

Components vary according to the design selected. The Solarium series includes a sealed and flashed sill, all-aluminum frames, factory-sealed insulated glass, a completely concealed condensation-control system with neoprene gaskets, polyvinyl extruded thermal breaks to prevent sweating on frames, a condensation weep system to evacuate water outside the sill—all materials for finished assembly. Options include heating and venting equipment, integral shades, with aluminum frames available in mill finish, white, or bronze.

MATERIALS

Lord & Burnham sills tie down with ½-inch bolts. The glazing bars are heavy-gauge aluminum, which the company reports reduces the flex found in other systems by 60 percent. Glazing is supported on all four edges by $3/16$-inch neoprene gaskets, and all glazing bars and horizontal mullions contain polyvinyl extrusions for continuous thermal breaks. The glazing bars weigh 1.4 pounds per running foot. The window greenhouse unit (all 17 inches deep) is prefab in widths and heights from 36 to 72 inches, with white or bronze frames. Glazing is ½-inch insulated glass. Venting is controlled with an interior wall knob to operate a sliding vent panel.

SPECIAL FEATURES

Solarium series energy specifications provide a U-factor of 0.57 for both glass and frame, an air infiltration rate of 0.08 CFM per square foot. The unit is engineered to maintain an inside humidity of 25 percent with outside temperature as low as −10°F.

RELATIVE SIZE/COST

Lord & Burnham window greenhouse units are approximately $350 for 36 x 36-inch modules, with a proportional increase up to $750 for the 72 x 72-inch module. Double-glazed Solarium units 5½ feet wide (for room extensions) are about $2,200 for 7½-foot lengths, up to $7,200 for 25-foot lengths, expandable in 2-foot-6-inch modules. The same model in 10-foot-6-inch widths (full room size) with optional wall connector package is about $2,600 for 7-foot-6-inch lengths, up to $9,000 for 25-foot lengths.

COMPANY INFORMATION

The firm ships nationally, and maintains three regional sales offices. A thirty-five-page full-color catalog is sent on request.

SUN SYSTEM PREFABRICATED SOLAR GREENHOUSES

60 Vanderbilt
Motor Parkway
Commack, NY 11725
(516) 543-7766
(800) 645-4506

PRODUCT RANGE

Sun System makes many stock plan greenhouses with angular eaves (a straight rafter line meets a vertical wall) and gracefully curved eaves (the rafter leg arcs down to meet a shorter vertical wall). Depths range from 3- to over 13-foot sections in both styles. Finished height at the high side of the roof (where the greenhouse would join an existing house) ranges from roughly 7 to 10 feet 6 inches. Gable-end height is roughly 4 feet 6 inches, and intended to rest on a knee wall.

PREFAB COMPONENTS

Sun System provides all materials to enclose the greenhouse space, including aluminum extrusions, precut and predrilled, and double-insulated ⅞-inch tempered and laminated safety glass, built-in weep systems to carry off condensation, hardware, sidewall glass, awning window vents. Accessories include climate control systems, watering systems (if you actually use the space as a greenhouse instead of as a sun-room), and a variety of manual and automatic shade systems.

MATERIALS

Aluminum extrusions are .090 gauge, 1.2 pounds per foot with .125 gauge on larger models. All hardware is stainless steel, maintaining a continuous thermal break. This stops direct temperature transfer through solid metal from outside to inside. Straight eave models are pitched 4 in 12.

SPECIAL FEATURES

Completely precut and predrilled Sun System kits can be installed over an existing slab in one day, using self-supporting lean-to

frames fixed between house wall and slab, then setting glass panels into weatherstripped seams that tighten down with a screwdriver.

RELATIVE SIZE/COST

Prices are quoted on request from one of the 250-odd Sun System dealers in the United States and Canada. A 3-bay model roughly 8 feet long enclosing 234 square feet is approximately $4,400. A 12-bay unit 31 feet long enclosing 552 square feet is roughly $9,600, with a $1,200 option for solar bronze roof glass. Vented Sun System window greenhouse enclosures are $375 for a 35 x 35-inch opening, and $560 for a 3 x 6-foot opening.

COMPANY INFORMATION

Sun System is a division of Kapco Development, Inc., a construction company in business since 1932. The firm operates nationally. After an order is placed with a deposit the company will provide a rendering of the base structure size and full specs for site preparation.

Construction details of Sun System greenhouses

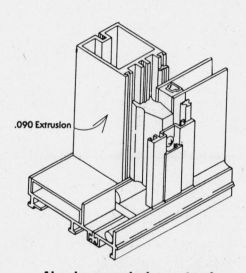

Aluminum main bar extrusions

.090 Extrusion

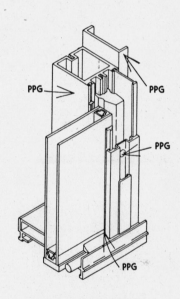

PPG enamel finish

PPG

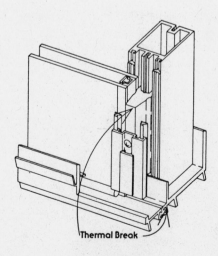

Thermal Break

Thermal breaks

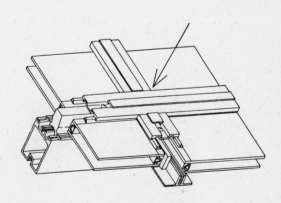

Overhead glass

VEGETABLE FACTORY, INC.

Solar Structures Division
71 Vanderbilt Avenue
New York, NY 10169
(212) 867-0113

PRODUCT RANGE

The Vegetable Factory makes attractive lean-to greenhouses 3 to 12 feet wide in 4-foot modules, and freestanding models 8 to 24 feet wide in 4-foot modules. Between frame patterns with low eaves, expansive, two-story facades, and various rafter angles, it is possible to fabricate a wide array of designs.

PREFAB COMPONENTS

The Vegetable Factory offers complete kits with a good selection of doors and vents, all-aluminum framework and connecting hardware, both passive and active solar systems, and many interesting options—for example, their Solar-Pod, which is a storage system of factory-sealed crystalline (phase-change) filled panels. The salt hydrate in the pods (48 inches wide, 16 inches high, and 2 inches thick) liquefies at 81°F. and absorbs heat. Each pod stores 2,200 BTUs.

MATERIALS

All frame components are extruded aluminum with a bronze finish. Solar panels are acrylic/fiber glass rigid glazing, a true sandwich panel of two clear sheets for double-glazed energy efficiency. A one-inch dead-air space is maintained between panels, which are permanently bonded to a rigid alu-

minum frame. The frames are attached to a mounting flange for installation in the structural framework.

SPECIAL FEATURES
High energy efficiency is maintained at points where insulated panels join the structural frame with a thermal break system. PVC foam gaskets interrupt temperature transfer from metal to metal, and into the greenhouse. For energy number crunchers, the panels have a U-factor of 0.50, and an R-value of 2.00, an improvement over insulated glass. The company emphasizes do-it-yourself possibilities by providing a very simple system of stakes and anchor bolts for setting the aluminum sill directly on a compacted base without an expensive concrete foundation.

RELATIVE SIZE/COST
Modest, lean-to greenhouses (roughly 5½ feet wide, 8 feet long, and 8 feet high) are approximately $2,000. Company literature includes a cost comparison chart covering roughly 100-square-foot greenhouses from five competitors (with a low-end price of $4,800 and a high-end price of $7,500) and the Vegetable Factory's model at $3,600; $32 per square foot.

COMPANY INFORMATION
Voluminous literature includes detailed energy-saving computations and case histories, booklets of measured plans and components, a full-color booklet showing many installations and styles, plus details of d-i-y glazing panels you can install on a wood-frame greenhouse of your own design and construction. The firm asks for $2 to cover inquiry costs.

COMPLETE-IT-YOURSELF HOMES

CURTIS HOMES, INC.
2201 Florida Avenue S
Minneapolis, MN 55426
(612) 542-4300

PRODUCT RANGE
Curtis is a unique company offering fifty "complete-it-yourself" homes. Every package contains all the necessary materials to create a finished house, down to heating plants and light fixtures. Curtis crews generally erect the basic frame, and then the owners complete the job. Although other prefab firms operate the same way, Curtis designs and builds specifically for families who can qualify for home ownership with sweat equity as part of the down payment. Homes in many styles range from small starter houses under 1,000 square feet to two-story homes over 2,500 square feet with four bedrooms, two and a half baths, and double garage. Modifications are allowed on all plans.

PREFAB COMPONENTS
A typical Curtis job is started by company crews who close in the home on an owner-prepared foundation, installing sills, walls, insulated sheathing and subfloor, steel corner bracing, rafters and collar ties, roof decking and felt paper, windows and doors, partition walls, and stairs. Owners take over inside with wall insulation, vapor barrier, and wallboard. Curtis provides everything needed for the job, such as metal corner bead, tape, and joint compound for walls. Standard packages include all exterior millwork, closet shelving, finished stairs, trim, and ⁵/₈-inch underlayment. Owners install cabinets, heating, plumbing, and electrical systems, working from detailed assembly manuals.

MATERIALS
Curtis offers many name-brand material options. Basic packages include double headers and top plates, clear, kiln-dried, treated ponderosa pine windows with storms and screens. Wall construction includes a 4-mil polyethylene vapor barrier with WR wallboard for tub and shower areas. Standard kitchen cabinets are flush oak veneer and prefinished.

SPECIAL FEATURES
Curtis has worked out highly specialized financing plans to get owners started with little or no down payment. Their Construction Credit Plan includes features such as interest-only payments during construction, delayed first payment (up to six months), time to complete the house and shop for permanent financing, and more. These homes qualify for FHA and VA loans. As with any major financial commitment, you should always comparison-shop for the best terms and rates.

RELATIVE SIZE/COST
One of Curtis's larger models, the Bonaventure, with about 2,400 square feet, can be financed several ways. With no down payment, twenty total payments start at $530 for the first eight months, and escalate to $681 for the last twelve months. The home costs roughly $12,500, which translates to $5 per square foot for the construction package. Of course this price excludes land, septic system, excavation, foundation, and other site costs.

COMPANY INFORMATION
Curtis will quote total cost, and break down finance options for any model with your modifications. A full information packet includes articles on Curtis in *Mechanix Illustrated* (September 1983), now *Home Mechanix*, plus details of construction and financing plans.

POD HOMES

TOPSIDER HOMES, TANGLEWOOD MANUFACTURING, INC.

Highway 601, P.O. Box 849
Yadkinville, NC 27055
(919) 679-8846

PRODUCT RANGE

Topsider makes unique pedestal-base octagonal modules, economically framed with 800 to 1,000 square feet of floor space above a ground-level support core with enough room for an entryway and circular-stair access to the living level. Three mini-shell models are also offered, providing roughly 465 and 565 square feet. Modular pedestal pods may be installed over full-height octagonal foundations and joined with a common wall or connecting room to make larger homes of multiple octagonal units.

PREFAB COMPONENTS

Topsider packages include roof and floor trusses (one with peak up and one with peak down, to leave living space with flat floor and ceiling in between), hardware fasteners, prefab floor and exterior wall panels, windows and doors, all inside wiring and electrical fixtures, plus steel spiral stairs for access from the ground-level pedestal. An extensive number of options includes complete plumbing, full kitchens, and complete interior finishing.

MATERIALS

Built around a center pedestal beam (a 6-inch-square column of ¼-inch-thick steel), living space is spanned with Douglas fir or southern yellow pine trusses supported by 6 x 6-inch wood posts at outside walls. Roof panels, which mount directly to the trusses, are made of 2 x 6-inch frames with ½-inch CDX plywood on top, and ¼-inch AC plywood on the bottom, covered with a narrow-weave fabric. Between finished panels, insulation (6 inches of fiber glass) and a vapor barrier provide climate control. Prefab flooring panels are made with ⅝-inch subflooring and ⅜-inch exposed sheathing. Windows are double-glazed safety glass.

SPECIAL FEATURES

Topsider's pedestal design provides unique appearance and efficient elevated living space. The design is versatile enough to be used with a full-octagon ground-level floor for roughly 2,000 square feet of total living space. These pod buildings have been used at Walt Disney World and Hilton Head and Pinehurst resorts.

RELATIVE SIZE/COST

The basic pedestal shell with 1,000 square feet is approximately $23,000, with spiral stairs to ground-level enclosure roughly $26,000. Full, two-story duplex models with 1,800 square feet are roughly $30,000; $17 per square foot.

COMPANY INFORMATION

Topsider's color brochure includes several interior and exterior views, with plan and elevation drawings to give you an idea of possible layouts in an octagonal space. Brochures are sent on request.

POLE HOMES

POLE HOUSE KITS OF CALIFORNIA

220 Newport Center Drive
No. 10, Design Plaza
Newport Beach, CA 92660
(714) 720-0499

PRODUCT RANGE

Pole House Kits of California is the only firm offering precut homes built on full-round poles. Pole building has been used in maritime construction, to elevate structures above the water, and in utility farm construction. The system was first used for residential building in California in the 1950s to rescue steeply sloped building sites not suitable for conventional construction. The company offers ten different models, including a brand-new one called the Nara Gatehouse. The models range from about 600 to nearly 4,000 square feet. The homes are uniformly expansive, with wide-open interiors and spacious, wraparound verandas.

PREFAB COMPONENTS

Pole House kits include a grid of 12- to 14-inch-diameter poles, heavy dimensional timber floor and roof framing, veranda deck and railings, exterior walls with solid redwood interior and exterior paneling and trim, roof deck ready for finishing, prehung interior and exterior doors with etched-glass fanlight panels, stairs and steps, plus all pole assembly hardware. Options include glazed roofing tile from Japan and elegant Poggenpohl kitchen and bath cabinets.

MATERIALS

Building poles are ponderosa pine or Douglas fir, Wolmanized (pressure-treated with a copper salt preservative). Subflooring is ¾-inch CCX t&g plywood with select oak-finished flooring. Veranda decking is clear heart redwood. Exterior siding is ½ x 8 shiplap kiln-dried heart redwood or similar material with tongue and groove joints inside. Finished ceilings are tight-knot t&g spruce. Exterior doors are solid oak.

SPECIAL FEATURES

These pole buildings produce uncluttered interior space with floor and roof framing pinned to massive girders, which in turn are pinned to the pole grid set with 14- or 16-foot spacing. Full-height poles can be set to provide single-level living space on the steepest, most inaccessible sites.

RELATIVE SIZE/COST

Call or write for specific price quotes. But as a guide, the company's new model, the four-pole Nara Gatehouse with roughly 600 square feet, has an estimated price of $30,000 for the deluxe package, including glazed roof tile, imported cabinets, solid oak stairs, and other options; roughly $50 per square foot for the finished house.

COMPANY INFORMATION

Pole House Kits presents their pole designs in a carefully detailed brochure for $7.

REPRODUCTION HOMES

BOW HOUSE, INC.
Bolton, MA 01740
(617) 779-6464
1-401-454-8433

PRODUCT RANGE
Bow House makes several variations of a very basic Cape design with a very special roof line. It's called an extant bowed roof. The first one was built by a shipwright in 1678, and resembles a gracefully curved boat hull turned upside down above the frame walls. Their stock plans range from a small quarter Cape with 1,182 square feet, through half and three-quarter Capes, to a full Cape with 2,563 square feet. Bow House also makes several garage/barn structures (roughly 24 x 24 feet), and a restrained line of gazebos and other garden structures.

PREFAB COMPONENTS
Bow House kits are architectural packages. Company literature explains clearly that the owner prepares a foundation, structural and subfloor, as well as frame walls and sheathing—really most of a frame house. Bow House takes over once you have framed to plan specifications, providing the distinctive laminated roof rafters and rake boards, plus standard kit items such as 16-inch white cedar shingles, ½ x 6-inch red cedar clapboard, copper rain diverter (you just don't find copper flashing in homes today, much less in kit homes), all windows and doors, trim, stair parts, forged interior hardware, handmade shutters, and more—an architectural finishing, closing-in package.

MATERIALS
Bow House stock materials include wide-board 1 x 12 pine flooring, bead-edged base molding, hand-forged shutter dogs and thumb-latch door hardware, and some truly unusual details such as hand-blown glass in 12-over-12-light double-hung windows. There are some interesting options, although almost all of the authentic goodies are standard, like the handmade 1¾-inch-thick clear pine panel entry door with bull's-eye glass lights. Down to the smallest detail, Bow House design and materials make a new but authentic and carefully detailed early Colonial home.

RELATIVE SIZE/COST
Architectural packages for a quarter Cape are about $20,000 ($17 per square foot), with estimated total construction cost of $60,000 to $70,000. Packages for full Capes are roughly $31,000 ($14 per square foot), with total costs estimated at $115,000 to $125,000, depending on site, season, and other variables.

COMPANY INFORMATION
Bow House's artwork, after the style of Eric Sloane (actually drawn by Charlie Wilton), is an interesting and inviting way to present a well-detailed house. The modest but elegant Bow House literature is clear and concise about what an architectural package is and just what is left to the owner.

STEEL-FRAME HOMES

PARAGON STEEL STRUCTURES, INC.

4131 East Wood Street
Phoenix, AZ 85040
(602) 243-5228

PRODUCT RANGE

Paragon offers many designs built around a modified U-shape super-structure of steel beams. Like a ship's hull turned upside down on a conventional foundation, these frames are freestanding. Paragon is based in Phoenix, and many of their stock plans (customized options are available) have a distinctly southwestern style, with terracotta, Mission-style roofs.

PREFAB COMPONENTS

Paragon building packages are designed to bolt together on-site, and the company literature suggests easy do-it-yourself assembly. Kits include the steel super-structure with second-floor support joists, steel rafters, and purlins; all bolts and fasteners; corrugated steel sheathing with self-tapping fasteners; a corrugated steel roof deck that conceals the framing system; a 9-inch fiber glass blanket (R-30) throughout the structure; end walls with 2 x 8 studs 24 inches on center; plywood truss joists; and all interior furring strips to hold finished wallboard, paneling, or other inside surface.

MATERIALS

Steel sheathing over framing is 26-gauge, interlocking and corrugated; 24-gauge is used on the roof deck with a baked-on finish. A wide variety of materials is available, including Texture 1-11 exterior siding, which helps to give many of Paragon's homes an efficient, modern look.

SPECIAL FEATURES

The prefab steel frame system offers several advantages: a continuous R-30 insulating blanket, freestanding exterior wall structure permitting any arrangement of partition walls, and thermal break material between steel columns and sheathing.

RELATIVE SIZE/COST

Specific prices are quoted on request, although the company estimates that the steel frame prefabrication saves 30 percent of conventional construction costs. The average 1,200-square-foot Paragon house sells for about $14,000; $11.50 per square foot.

COMPANY INFORMATION

Paragon provides an interesting brochure showing several of their standard plans, which look very much like conventionally framed houses.

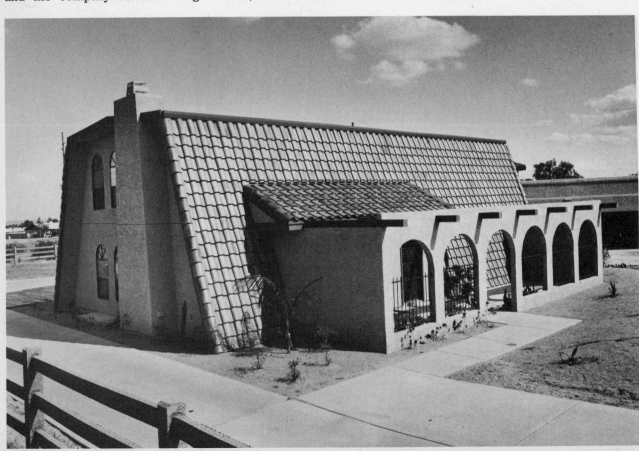

TRI-STEEL STRUCTURES, INC.
1400 Crescent
Denton, TX 76201
(817) 566-1386

PRODUCT RANGE
Tri-Steel uses a basic frame design (a kind of splayed U-shape) as a backbone of many plans ranging from 600 to 6,000 square feet. Although the frame system is uniform from house to house, different types of siding, windows, and a variety of porch and dormer designs allow variations on the U-shape, which can be a bit stark all on its own.

PREFAB COMPONENTS
Standard packages include the steel frame shipped in bolt-together sections, steel roof panels and siding (several options include wood shakes, and Alcoa aluminum shakes, which are standard on many models), bolt connections between steel columns and piers or a concrete slab, standard Texture-111 gable end-wall siding, 16-inch center 2 x 4 furring strips for wallboard and

paneling application, and 9½-inch insulation to yield an R-30 wall.

MATERIALS

Anticipating consumers' reluctance to attempt custom steel framing, all frame members are shipped precut. All siding and roofing includes mastic and fasteners. Standard sheeting is 26-gauge steel available in twelve colors. End-wall framing is 2 x 6 studs with Texture-111 siding and 6-inch fiber glass batts (R-19). R-30 batts are standard elsewhere. Design options include framed sundeck extensions, carports, garages, and custom dormers.

SPECIAL FEATURES

Tri-Steel asserts that their pre-engineered homes (they prefer that to "prefab") can be erected by owner-builders without special equipment. Prepunched bolt holes make frame assembly fast, and the company notes "you're basically working with a giant erector set." Take four to six days to complete a slab, then approximately five to eight days to erect the steel frame, install insulation, and cover with siding.

RELATIVE SIZE/COST

Sample models include a 1,024-square-foot Hillcrest model for roughly $18,000 ($17.50 per foot), and an interesting option for owner-investors (a very new breed) called the Heritage. It's a four-family building, about 30 x 72 feet, providing four 1,080-square-foot units. The cost is roughly $40,000.

COMPANY INFORMATION

Tri-Steel homes from 600 to 6,000 square feet include plans that meet FHA and VA requirements. The firm is the nation's largest manufacturer of steel-frame homes. Company crews can travel to most areas of the country to erect the steel shell if need be. Delivery is within four or five weeks.

Construction details of a Tri-Steel home

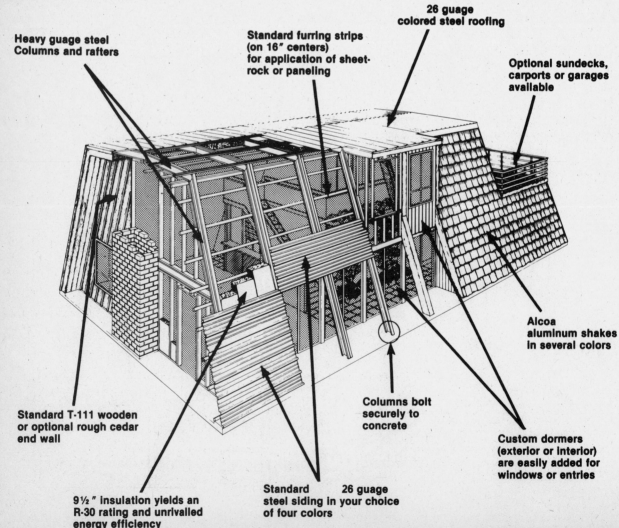

Heavy guage steel Columns and rafters

Standard furring strips (on 16″ centers) for application of sheet-rock or paneling

26 guage colored steel roofing

Optional sundecks, carports or garages available

Alcoa aluminum shakes in several colors

Standard T-111 wooden or optional rough cedar end wall

Columns bolt securely to concrete

Custom dormers (exterior or interior) are easily added for windows or entries

9½″ insulation yields an R-30 rating and unrivalled energy efficiency

Standard 26 guage steel siding in your choice of four colors

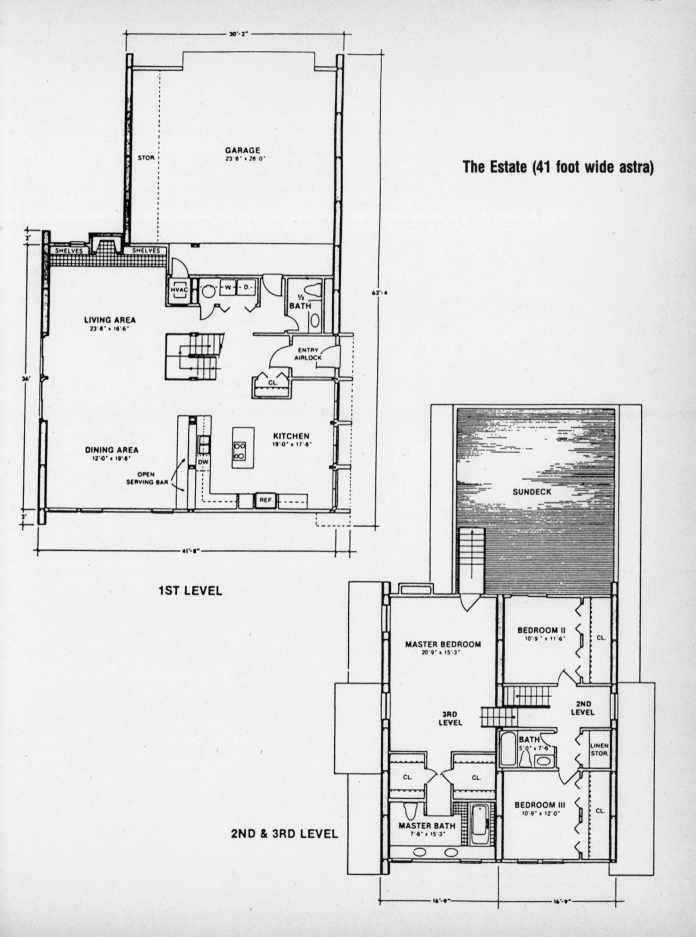

The Estate (41 foot wide astra)

GARAGE
23'-6" x 28'-0"

STOR.

SHELVES   SHELVES

HVAC   W.   D.   ½ BATH

LIVING AREA
23'-8" x 16'-6"

ENTRY AIRLOCK

CL.

DINING AREA
12'-0" x 19'-8"

OPEN SERVING BAR

DW

KITCHEN
19'-0" x 17'-8"

REF

1ST LEVEL

SUNDECK

MASTER BEDROOM
20'-9" x 15'-3"

BEDROOM II
10'-9" x 11'-6"

CL.

3RD LEVEL

2ND LEVEL

BATH
5'-0" x 7'-6"

LINEN STOR.

CL.   CL.

BEDROOM III
10'-9" x 12'-0"

CL.

2ND & 3RD LEVEL

MASTER BATH
7'-6" x 15'-3"

LIST OF MANUFACTURERS

LOG HOMES
Air-Lock Log Company, Inc.
Alta Industries, Ltd.
American Lincoln Homes
Appalachian Log Structures
Authentic Homes Corp.
Beaver Log Homes
Gastineau Log Homes
Greatwood Log Homes, Inc.
Green Mountain Log Homes
Green River Trading Co.
Heritage Log Homes
Heritage Solid Wood Homes
Log Structures of the South
New England Log Homes, Inc.
Northern Products
   Log Homes, Inc.
Rocky Mountain Log Homes
Southern Cypress
   Log Homes, Inc.
Southland Log Homes, Inc.
Wilderness Log Homes, Inc.

POST AND BEAM HOMES
American Timber Homes, Inc.
Deck House, Inc.
Fox-Maple Post & Beam
Habitat American Barn
Pacific Frontier Homes, Inc.
Shelter-Kit, Inc.
Solar Northern
   Post & Beam, Inc.
Timberpeg
Timber Systems, Inc.
Wickes Lumber
Yankee Barn Homes

MANUFACTURED HOMES
Acorn Structures, Inc.
Cardinal Industries, Inc.
DeLuxe Homes of
   Pennsylvania, Inc.
Fleetwood Enterprises, Inc.
Galaxy Homes, Inc.
Marley Continental Homes
Nationwide Homes, Inc.
North American Housing Corp.
Northern Homes
Pacific Buildings, Inc.
Redman Homes, Inc.

PANELIZED HOMES
Affordable Luxury Homes, Inc.
American Standard Homes Corp.
Chase Barlow Lumber Co.
Delta Industries, Inc.
Deltec Homes
Haida Hide, Inc.
Northern Counties Lumber, Inc.
Pacific Modern Homes, Inc.
True Value Homes

DOME HOMES
Aluminum Geodesic Spheres
Daystar Shelter Corp.
Dome Creations
Domes America
Domiciles, Inc.
Geodesic Domes, Inc.
Geodesic Homes
Monterey Domes
Natural Spaces, Inc.
Timberline Geodesics, Inc.

TIMBER-WALL HOMES
Cedar Forest Products Co.
Justus Log Homes
Pan Abode Cedar Homes
Pre-Cut International
   Homes, Inc.

EARTH-SHELTERED HOMES
Terra-Dome Corp.

GREENHOUSES
Garden Way SunRoom/Solar
   Greenhouse
Lord & Burnham, Division
   Burnham Corp.
Sun System Prefabricated Solar
   Greenhouses
Vegetable Factory, Inc.

COMPLETE-IT-YOURSELF HOMES
Curtis Homes, Inc.

POD HOMES
Topsider Homes, Tanglewood
   Manufacturing, Inc.

POLE-HOMES
Pole House Kits of California

REPRODUCTION HOMES
Bow House, Inc.

STEEL-FRAME HOMES
Paragon Steel Structures, Inc.
Tri-Steel Structures, Inc.

PHOTO/ILLUSTRATION ACKNOWLEDGMENTS

Picture credits are listed by page number.

6 Photograph courtesy of Air-Lock Company, Inc.
7 Photograph courtesy of Alta Industries, Ltd.
8–9 Photographs courtesy of American Lincoln Homes
10 Spencer model photograph courtesy of Appalachian Log Structures
11 Photograph courtesy of Authentic Homes Corp.
12 Photograph courtesy of Beaver Log Homes
13–14 Photographs courtesy of Gastineau Log Homes
15 Photograph courtesy of Greatwood Log Homes, Inc.
16 Photograph courtesy of Green Mountain Log Homes
17 Saltbox photograph courtesy of Green River Trading Co.
18 Photograph courtesy of Heritage Log Homes
19 Photograph courtesy of Heritage Solid Wood Homes
20 Photograph courtesy of Log Structures of the South
21 Photograph © 1980 by NELHI. All rights reserved. Used by permission New England Log Homes, Inc.
22 Photograph courtesy of Northern Products Log Homes, Inc.
23–24 Photographs courtesy of Rocky Mountain Log Homes
25 Photograph courtesy of Southern Cypress Log Homes, Inc.
26 Photograph by Crewe. Courtesy of Southland Log Homes, Inc.
27 Photograph courtesy of Wilderness Log Homes, Inc.
30 Vista Sportsman photograph copyright by American Timber Homes, Inc.
31 Country Squire photograph copyright by American Timber Homes, Inc.
32 Conservatory House photograph courtesy of Deck House, Inc.
33 Conservatory House photograph courtesy of Deck House, Inc. Photograph by Fred Rola
34 Photograph courtesy of Fox-Maple Post & Beam
35 American Barn I photograph courtesy of Habitat American Barn
36 Passive Solar 2 photograph courtesy of Habitat American Barn
37 "Eagle's Nest" at Sea Ranch on Northern California Coast photograph courtesy of Pacific Frontier Homes, Inc.
38 Unit One photograph courtesy of Shelter-Kit, Inc.

39 2,500 Square Foot custom designed home photograph courtesy of Solar Northern Post & Beam, Inc.
40 Interior view of 2-story Saltbox photograph courtesy of Solar Northern Post & Beam, Inc.
41–42 Photographs courtesy of Timberpeg
43 Photograph copyright © 1984 by TSI. All rights reserved. Used by permission of Timber Systems, Inc.
44 Photographs courtesy of Wickes Lumber
45 Floor plan courtesy of Wickes Lumber
46 Photograph courtesy of Yankee Barn Homes
48 Solar Series 2700 photograph by Barth Falkenberg. Courtesy of Acorn Structures, Inc.
49 Floor plans of Solar Series 2700 courtesy of Acorn Structures, Inc.
50 Photograph copyright © 1984 by Cardinal Industries, Inc. All rights reserved. Used by permission of Cardinal Industries, Inc.
51 Drawings courtesy of Deluxe Homes of Pennsylvania, Inc.
52–53 Photographs courtesy of Fleetwood Enterprises, Inc.
54 Photograph courtesy of Galaxy Homes, Inc.
55 Photograph copyright © 1984 by Bob Raiche. All rights reserved. Used by permission of Marley Continental Homes.
57 Photographs courtesy of Nationwide Homes, Inc.
58 Photograph courtesy of North American Housing Corp.
59–60 Photographs courtesy of Northern Homes
61 Photograph courtesy of Pacific Buildings, Inc.
63 Photograph courtesy of Redman Homes, Inc.
66 Front elevation courtesy of Affordable Luxury Homes
67 Photographs courtesy of Affordable Luxury Homes
68 George Taylor Model photograph courtesy of American Standard Homes Corp.
69 Photograph courtesy of Chase Barlow Lumber Co.
70 Photograph courtesy of Delta Industries, Inc.
71–72 Photographs by William G. Frank. Courtesy of Rochester Museum and Science Center, 657 E. Ave., Box 1480, Rochester, NY
73 24-foot-wide Cedar Chalet photographs courtesy of Haida Hide, Inc.
74 Photograph by Al Whitley, Whitley and Associates. Courtesy of Northern Counties Lumber, Inc.
75 Photograph courtesy of Northern Counties Lumber, Inc.
76 Photograph courtesy of Pacific Modern Homes, Inc.
77 Floor plans courtesy of Pacific Modern Homes, Inc.

78 Photograph courtesy of True Value Homes
79 Floor plans courtesy of True Value Homes
82 Fiberglass home in the Florida keys photograph courtesy of Aluminum Geodesic Spheres
83 Photograph courtesy of Aluminum Geodesic Spheres
84 Photograph courtesy of Daystar Shelter Corp.
85 Photograph courtesy of Dome Creations
86 Photograph and floor plan courtesy of Dome Creations
87 Photograph courtesy of Domes America
88 Photograph by Harry E. Boll, Davenport, Iowa. Courtesy of Domiciles, Inc.
89 Photograph and floor plan courtesy of Geodesic Domes, Inc.
90 Photograph courtesy of Geodesic Homes
91–92 Photographs courtesy of Monterey Domes
93 Photograph courtesy of Natural Spaces, Inc.
94 Floor plans courtesy of Natural Spaces, Inc.
95 Photograph courtesy of Natural Spaces, Inc.
96 Photograph courtesy of Timberline Geodesics, Inc.
98 Floor plan courtesy of Cedar Forest Products Co.
99 Photo courtesy of Cedar Forest Products Co.
100 Photograph courtesy of Justus Log Homes
101 Photograph courtesy of Pan Adobe Cedar Homes
102–103 Photographs courtesy of Pre-Cut International Homes, Inc.
106–107 Photographs courtesy of Terra-Dome Corp.
110 Photograph courtesy of Garden Way Sunroom/Solar Greenhouse
111 Photograph by Robert Perron. Courtesy of Lord & Burnham, Division Burnham Corp.
112 Photograph courtesy of Sun System Prefabricated Solar Greenhouses
113 Construction detail illustrations courtesy of Sun System Prefabricated Solar Greenhouse
114–115 Photographs courtesy of Vegetable Factory, Inc.
118 Photograph courtesy of Curtis Homes, Inc.
120 Photograph courtesy of Topsider Homes, Tanglewood Manufacturing, Inc.
122–123 Photographs courtesy of Pole House Kits of California
126 Photograph courtesy of Bow House, Inc.
128 Photograph by Mallory's Commercial Photographs. Courtesy of Paragon Steel Structures, Inc.
129 Photographs copyright © 1983 by Tri-Steel Structures, Inc. All rights reserved. Used by permission of Tri-Steel Structures, Inc.
130–131 Construction details illustrations and floor plans copyright © 1983 by Tri-Steel Structures, Inc. All rights reserved. Used by permission of Tri-Steel Structures, Inc.